Other Very Short Stories

Paul Stewart

PENGUIN BOOKS

PENGUIN BOOKS

Published by the Penguin Group
Penguin Books Ltd, 27 Wrights Lane, London w8 5tz, England
Penguin Books USA Inc., 375 Hudson Street, New York, New York 10014, USA
Penguin Books Australia Ltd, Ringwood, Victoria, Australia
Penguin Books Canada Ltd, 10 Alcorn Avenue, Toronto, Ontario, Canada m4v 3b2
Penguin Books (NZ) Ltd, 182–190 Wairau Road, Auckland 10, New Zealand

Penguin Books Ltd, Registered Offices: Harmondsworth, Middlesex, England

First published in Penguin Books 1997
3 5 7 9 10 8 6 4 2

Text copyright © Paul Stewart, 1997
All rights reserved

The moral right of the author has been asserted

Phototypeset by Rowland Phototypesetting Ltd, Bury St Edmunds, Suffolk
Printed in England by Clays Ltd, St Ives plc
Set in 10.5/12.5pt Monophoto Plantin

Contents

Introduction   v

Pluto   1
The Bad Prawn   7
Lucky Luke   12
Dining Out   17
The Abyss   23
Mr Armitage   28
The Final Memo   33
Fireworks   38
The Shikara Man   44
'Patata'   50
Origami   55
Memory Lane   61

Glossary and Language Practice   66

Introduction

'What can I do to improve my English?' When foreign language learners ask this question, it is time for them to move away from text books and start reading on their own.

A text book can give a foreign language learner a grounding in the basics of the new grammar, as well as a basic vocabulary. To develop a 'feel' for the language, however, it is important to read authentic material. The question is, what sort of authentic material?

Newspapers are often too idiomatic; novels, too long; and poems and plays, too difficult. What the language learner needs is something to read that is:

- a good read! – the sort of book you might read in your own language;
- not too long! – you should be able to finish reading it in one go;
- natural! – it should be written in everyday English, with idioms and expressions;
- helpful! – there should be explanations of the new language, and exercises, to give you a chance to use that new language.

The short stories in this collection are set in a variety of locations around the world, from Lanzarote to Sri Lanka. Some are funny, some are sad, some, I hope, will make you think. All of them are about people and what makes them tick.

I hope you enjoy them.

Pluto

Vicky was prepared for everything. She always had a pen
in her bag if you needed one, and she could stitch back a
button immediately if it came off. So, of course, when
Emma's heel broke off her shoe, Vicky just took a tube of
glue from her pocket and stuck it back on.   5

'Forty-two pounds, they cost me,' Emma complained.

Vicky nodded as she blew on the heel. 'You should get
some of these,' she said.

Emma looked at Vicky's lace-up boots, and smiled. 'I
don't think so,' she said.   10

No, thought Vicky. Their footwear showed the differences between the two girls. Emma Miles, with her high
heels – and her head in the clouds. And Vicky Reynolds
with her heavy-booted feet firmly on the ground.

'I hate this place,' Emma shuddered.   15

'Why?' said Vicky, surprised. Elm Walk was a short-cut
to the centre of town – she'd never really noticed it before.

'Because it's creepy,' said Emma.

Vicky looked up and down the road. There were bungalows on both sides. All of them were designed for people   20
who – for one reason or another – could not climb stairs.
Elm Walk was always a quiet street. Now, at half past eight
in the evening, it was silent. Vicky noticed, however, that
she and Emma were not alone. There was someone behind
every single net-curtain, watching them.   25

'Nosey old . . . !' Emma said angrily.

'They're lonely,' said Vicky. She looked back at the row of half-hidden faces. 'We're probably the most exciting thing that's happened all day. There,' she said, handing Emma her shoe. 'Try that.'

The heel was as good as new. Ten minutes later Vicky and Emma were standing in front of Stacey's Disco.

'Here again, girls?' said the man on the cloakroom desk, when they checked in their coats.

'Of course we are, Harv,' said Emma. 'It's Friday night!'

As the door opened, a blast of heat, light and noise struck them. Even though Vicky went to Stacey's every Friday night, it was always a shock. 'Drink?' she heard Emma shouting in her ear.

'Yes, please,' she yelled back.

They crossed the dance floor to the bar, with Emma striding ahead. She held her head high, and pretended not to notice who was and wasn't there that evening. Vicky knew that she was probably also sucking in her cheeks. This made her cheek-bones stand out. Emma was very proud of her cheek-bones. By the time the drinks came, she was already lost in giggly conversation with a rugby player she knew, called Jeff.

Vicky sighed, sipped from her glass and wondered whether to buy a pair of high heels after all. 'The trouble is,' she thought, 'high heels attract the type of man who *likes* women in high heels,' – and that was exactly the type of man Vicky tried to avoid. She looked round. The disco was full of them: good-looking, well-dressed, sporty – and dull. 'Stacey's! I don't know why I bother,' she said, and checked the time.

At least, that was what she meant to do. Unfortunately, as she raised her arm to look at her watch, Vicky knocked the elbow of the man standing next to her. Although he managed not to drop his glass, he spilt his drink all down his front. He spun round.

'I'm so sorry!' Vicky exclaimed as, red and embarrassed, she searched her pockets for the tissues that she knew were there somewhere. 'Here we are,' she said at last, and began 65 dabbing furiously at his wet T-shirt.

'It's all right,' the man laughed. 'Honest.'

'I'll get you another drink,' said Vicky. 'What was it?'

The man looked at her. His eyes were the darkest blue Vicky had ever seen. They seemed to be looking right inside 70 her. 'Water,' he said softly. 'It was only water.' He looked down and pulled the wet cloth away from his chest.

For the first time, Vicky noticed the picture on the T-shirt. It was a humpback whale leaping out of the sea; beneath it, in blood red letters, the words SAVE ME! 75

'I'm surprised they let you in,' she said. 'T-shirt and jeans and that . . .' She stopped. 'I'm Vicky, by the way.'

'I'm Peter,' he said. 'Though most people call me Pluto.'

'Why?' said Vicky. 'No, don't tell me; because you're 80 dark and mysterious.'

He smiled. 'My surname's Plotovsky.'

'Oh,' said Vicky, feeling very guilty.

'It's Estonian,' he added. 'Look, why don't I get something to drink and a couple of glasses. We could find 85 somewhere a bit quieter to talk.'

Vicky nodded. 'I'd like that,' she said.

They found an empty table at the far end of the disco and sat down opposite one another. As Vicky watched him filling the glasses, deep in thought, she began to think that 90 maybe 'Pluto' *was* the perfect nickname for him.

They talked about the ban on whale hunting, and dolphin-friendly tuna fishing; about ivory and rhino horn, nuclear testing and global warming. They discovered they were both vegetarians, both eighteen – and both single. He 95 was a Gemini, she, an Aquarian. On and on they talked, and not once did they run out of things to say.

As they shared ideas and swapped stories, Vicky felt more and more confident. She wasn't a crank! There were others out there who didn't laugh at her worries. Or if not *others*, at least there was *someone*: Pluto. He even agreed with her theory about the people on Elm Walk. 'Yeah, perhaps they live through others,' he said. 'Perhaps that's what they're doing when they watch the passers-by – looking for a friendly face to share an hour or two of conversation with.'

Vicky stared at him. 'What an odd thought,' she said.

'A dark and mysterious thought,' Pluto laughed. 'By the way,' he added. 'I think someone over there is trying to get your attention.'

Vicky turned to see Emma waving frantically from the exit. She was carrying their coats, and pointing theatrically at her watch. 'It's my friend, Emma,' said Vicky. 'We're late . . .'

Pluto nodded. 'I've got to go, too,' he said. 'Look, can I . . . Can I give you my telephone number?'

'Of course,' said Vicky, and took from her pocket a pen and some paper.

'You write it down,' he said. '509573 – and put *Pluto* so you don't forget whose number it is!'

Vicky smiled. 'I won't forget,' she said. 'Look, I've really enjoyed this evening.' She looked round again. 'I'll have to go – before Emma explodes! I'll call you!'

'Do that,' said Pluto.

'I will,' she called back over the music. 'I promise.'

Vicky didn't keep her promise. She decided to pay him a visit instead. She couldn't wait to see his face – and yet, as she lifted the knocker, she hesitated. What if Pluto wasn't in? What if he'd only given her his number to be polite? She looked round. Someone was watching her from the

4

window opposite. She tapped lightly at the door, and waited.

Practical as ever, Vicky had written down Pluto's phone number in her address book as soon as she came home from Stacey's. She wrote it under P; P for Peter Plotovsky 135
– P for Pluto. Then, unhappy that she had no address to fill in, she looked it up in the telephone directory. There was only one Plotovsky listed, and the number was the same. It must be the one. But the address; it was 45 Elm Walk! 140

'Why?' she asked herself for the umpteenth time. 'We talked about the road. Why didn't he say he lived there?'

The door was opened by a stout woman of fifty or so. Her grey hair was tied up in a thick bun. She nodded to Vicky. 'You are better to come in,' she said. Her east 145
European accent was strong and, as they stood in the hallway, Vicky had to concentrate hard to make out what the woman was telling her. Something about a drunken hit-and-run driver, and her Peter being knocked down on his way back from a Save the Whale meeting, ten years ago! 150
Vicky shook her head. She was confused. For once, Vicky Reynolds was not prepared.

'Stop it!' she cried.

The woman paused. 'Sorry to upset,' she said gruffly. 'But this man, two years in prison, he gets, and Peter, my 155
darling boy – paralysed. He is in prison for rest of his life.' She turned and opened the door behind her.

And there he was; older, but without doubt the same person. It was Pluto. He was sitting in a wheelchair staring out of the window. Mrs Plotovsky turned him round to 160
face Vicky. His mouth moved into a faint smile. Vicky felt uneasy.

'His face, he can move some,' Mrs Plotovsky explained. 'The rest . . .' She shrugged.

Vicky nodded. 'He's lifting his eyebrows,' she said. 165

'It is his way to beckon,' said Mrs Plotovsky. 'He wishes to say something to you.'

Vicky stepped forwards. Her heart was racing. This couldn't really be him. It just couldn't be! She bent down towards his mouth, and felt his warm breath against her ear.

'Pluto says thank-you,' he whispered.

The Bad Prawn

Like most other boys, John Palmer liked football, loud
music and films, and thought that Silvie Lindemann was
the most beautiful woman on earth. On his sixteenth birthday his parents got him tickets for his favourite programme,
It's Friday Night!, and John was over the moon. When he   5
discovered that Silvie Lindemann would be there, he nearly
passed out.

'Come on, then,' his dad called up the stairs. 'They won't
let us in if we're late.'

Friday nights were always bad for traffic. This particular   10
Friday was the worst John had ever seen it. They arrived at
the studio with two minutes to spare.

'Just in time,' said the uniformed man on the door.
He looked at John and winked. 'First time on telly,
is it?'   15

John nodded. 'It's my birthday treat,' he said.

The man laughed. 'Good for you,' he said. 'Take those
stairs and turn left, and you'll find yourself in the Hospitality Canteen. Help yourself to what you'd like.'

There were about a hundred other people in the room,   20
sipping drinks, chewing and chatting. John looked at all
the food. He wasn't hungry, but he did like prawns. He
picked up a *vol-au-vent* and bit into it. A voice from the
loudspeaker told them they had three minutes before the
programme started.   25

7

As John followed his parents to the door, he burped. The taste of oily prawn filled his mouth. It was horrible.

From his seat, John looked down at the stage. On television the scenery looked grand, with marble pillars and arches which filled the whole screen. Close up, it was all made of painted board, and stopped three metres up. The wild applause from the audience was not real, either. Every time the warm-up man told a joke, a woman with black hair held up cue-cards. CLAP, said one. LAUGH, said another. APPLAUD AND CHEER, instructed yet another.

John burped again. The taste in his mouth was revolting. One of the prawns must have been bad.

The host of the show was Dean Winters. He walked down the hardboard stairs to the sound of WILD APPLAUSE, introduced himself to the audience, told them they were all wonderful and promised an evening they would never forget. In three million homes around the country, people settled themselves down for another evening of *It's Friday Night!*

After a brief talk, interrupted by LAUGH, LAUGH LOUDER, and finally APPLAUD AND CHEER, Dean Winters took his seat. He introduced his first guest, a small, thin woman who was there to speak about her travels in the Amazon.

John didn't pay much attention. He started to feel sick, and only noticed the woman had gone when the sound of loud music started hammering inside his head. He was hot, shivery, and his stomach hurt.

As the music faded away, the warm-up man reappeared. 'Terrific!' he yelled. 'You can all relax for a couple of minutes now. They're showing adverts.'

John turned to his mum. 'I don't feel well,' he said.

Mrs Palmer put her hand on his forehead. 'You're burning up,' she said. 'Do you want to go?'

8

John smiled weakly. 'And miss Silvie Lindemann?' he said.

'Well, you let me know if you feel any worse,' she said, her voice becoming a whisper as the warm-up man returned.

'. . . four, three, two . . .' he counted. 'And LIVE!'

'Welcome back!' Dean grinned into the camera. 'And now, my friends, the moment *I've* been waiting for. LAUGH. Miss Silvie Lindemann!' WILD APPLAUSE.

John watched Silvie appear at the top of the steps. His head spun, and he closed his eyes. When he opened them again, Silvie was on the settee, legs crossed and smiling round at the audience. She was older than John had thought.

His stomach gurgled, and he burped again, as quietly as he could.

Down at the front, Dean asked his questions, and Silvie replied. Her answers were short and often funny. Sometimes, they would lead into a little story, as though she had just thought of it. John, who had read an interview with her in his *Film* magazine, already knew every reply by heart.

'And the film?' Dean was saying. 'Tell us about the film.'

'This film is the most exciting thing I've ever worked on,' Silvie replied, as John knew she would.

He wiped his forehead on his sleeve. He loosened his braces and undid the top button of his trousers. His stomach gurgled some more.

The end of the interview was greeted with more WILD APPLAUSE. It was time for the final act of the show.

'Ladies and gents,' Dean Winters announced. 'The great, the incredible, the one and only Pickpocket Pete!'

APPLAUD AND CHEER and WILD APPLAUSE.

'You, madame,' said Pickpocket, pointing to a woman in a blue dress. 'Your name is Felicity and you have a dog

9

called Buster. Am I right?' The woman nodded, and the audience clapped. 'And you, sir,' he said, looking down at a tall man in the front row. 'You were born on 28 January 1970. You live in Bondi and have a pilot's licence. Am I right?' The man also nodded, the audience cheered. 'And you, sir, with the green shirt, you have a baby granddaughter called Amy who was born on 12 April last year. Am I right?'

'No,' said the man quietly. 'It was my daughter. She died on that date.'

For a moment there was an awful silence. The camera returned to Pickpocket Pete. 'YEAH!' he cried. 'And a round of applause for our Joker of the Week!'

CLAP, LAUGH, APPLAUD AND CHEER, WILD APPLAUSE, the cue-cards appeared one after the other. On the stage, Pickpocket Pete pulled a purse, a wallet and a photograph from inside his jacket.

'Never trust a person who bumps into you in a crowded Hospitality Canteen,' he said, and winked at the camera. 'You never know what you might lose.' LAUGH. He threw the objects back to the three people in the audience. 'Now!' he said. 'I need a volunteer.'

'Here, here, here!' John heard someone calling. He looked round. It was his dad, and he was pointing at *him*. 'His name's John Palmer,' he was shouting. 'John Palmer.'

Pickpocket Pete raced up the aisle, pulled John from his seat and led him back to the stage. John stared round at the rows of grinning faces. They all seemed to be getting bigger and smaller at the same time. His head was pounding, sweat ran down his cheek.

'Hot, eh?' said Pickpocket Pete. 'Have a hankie.' The audience clapped. It was John's own handkerchief, which they had seen Pete removing from John's pocket. 'And comb your hair while you're about it,' said Pete, handing John his own comb.

The audience's laughter echoed round his head, the whole studio was starting to spin again. John wanted to be sick.

Pickpocket Pete held up something red. The audience was howling with laughter. My braces, John thought, and grabbed at his trousers. It was already too late. With the top button undone, they had slipped down to his ankles. There was no need for the cue-cards, the audience loved it.

John tripped and fell towards the chair and settee. He noticed the anxious smile on Silvie Lindemann's face. She looked even older this near. Her make-up was like a mask. John hit the floor with a thump.

The audience cheered and whistled.

Slowly, John pulled himself onto his knees. Silvie Lindemann was smiling down at him, so close now. John swallowed, but it was no good, his stomach was determined to get rid of that bad prawn.

'Aaaargh!' Silvie Lindemann screeched in horror as the young man with no trousers vomited over her legs.

John looked up and wiped his eyes. He felt better already. The audience went crazy. Everyone thought the whole thing was planned. Even Silvie Lindemann was grinning into the camera, as she wiped herself with a towel.

'I'm so sorry,' said John.

Silvie continued to smile her beautiful smile. 'Get lost, you disgusting little jerk,' she said, too softly for the microphone to hear.

John stared at her. Like the marble pillars, and like the audience excitement, Silvie Lindemann was a fake.

Sometimes, it can take a whole lifetime for a person to discover that everything is not what it seems. With John Palmer, it had taken only one bad prawn.

Lucky Luke

It was hot in town, very hot. It seemed global warming was
finally happening, and we all had to adapt. In my own
little way, I was doing just that. My long hair was far too
uncomfortable in the sweltering heat and so, for the first
5   time in five years, I was going to get it cut.

The barber's, Jimmy's, was empty. Jimmy himself was
sitting on one of the chairs, reading a newspaper. He looked
up as I walked in. 'Yes?' he said, wearily.

'Errm. I . . .'

10   His small eyes narrowed. 'Are you from the press?' he
said. 'Because if you are, you can clear off now.'

I stared at him. 'I just want a haircut,' I said.

He looked surprised. 'You do?' he said, and jumped up.
'Take a seat. I'm sorry I . . . I've been having a few problems
15   with reporters,' he said. The phone started ringing. Jimmy
ignored it. 'That's probably one of them now.' The phone
continued to ring. Jimmy sighed. 'Just sit down. I won't be
a minute.'

I sat in the red leather seat, and looked at my reflection
20   in the mirror. 'Five years!' I thought. The hair was down
to my shoulders, thick, dark and wet with sweat. From the
other side of the bead curtain I could hear Jimmy's voice
getting louder.

'And I've told you, "no comment!" . . . Yes . . . No . . .
25   That's none of your business!'

I looked along the shelf in front of me, at the sink and shower, the combs and scissors, at the newspaper! The tabloid headline said, JIMMY'S: THE WORST BARBER IN BRITAIN. Next to it was a photograph of the man himself, the man I was about to let loose on *my* hair. I heard Jimmy slam the telephone down. He burst into the room and caught me looking at the newspaper. His face fell. 'You don't want to believe everything you read,' he said.

'Maybe,' I said. 'But . . .'

'It's a long story,' he said. 'I'll tell you while I'm cutting your hair. If you don't like it, I won't charge,' he added.

It was a good offer. 'Go on then,' I said.

He fixed the nylon coverall round my neck. 'How would you like it?' he said. 'I can't wash it, I'm afraid. Water shortage, and all that . . .'

'I just want it nice and cool,' I said.

'Short, then,' he said. 'How short?'

I wasn't sure. 'I'll tell you when to stop,' I said.

As he lifted my hair with the comb, and snipped with the scissors, he seemed to know what he was doing. So far so good, I thought.

'Right, then,' he said. 'You want to know why the papers called me the worst barber in Britain?'

'I did wonder,' I said.

'It's all because of my brother,' he said. 'Lucky Luke.'

From the way he spoke his name, I could tell Jimmy didn't think much of his brother. 'Four years younger than me, he is, and lucky since the day that he was born. When we were kids, he always beat me at board games: ludo, snakes and ladders . . . The dice always landed on whatever number he needed, you know what I mean? And football; he was always scoring the winning goal! That's the sort of bloke he is. Lucky.' He stopped cutting. 'How's that?' he said.

13

'Shorter, please,' I said.

Jimmy started snipping again. 'I mean, take the way he looks. You'd never know we were brothers. He got Mum's little nose and chin, and her thick hair. What did I get? Dad's big nose and receding hairline, and Mum's piggy eyes!' He stopped again. 'What about that?' he asked.

My hair was still not short enough. It was the sort of haircut that politicians and vicars have. Besides, I wanted to hear more of the story.

'A bit more off the sides, I think,' I said.

'As a teenager, I had various jobs,' Jimmy continued. 'Paper round, Saturday work in a butcher's, washing cars. Not Luke, though. He was so good-looking he got modelling work, didn't he? Sweets, jeans, you name it, he's advertised it. He made a fortune! Though nothing compared to what he's earning now!' Jimmy added bitterly. He stopped once more. 'How about *that*?'

I looked up. For the first time in years, I could actually see my ears. What was more, they felt cool! 'Just a bit more off the top and front,' I said.

Jimmy lifted and snipped. 'Of course, Luke inherited Mum's brains. She's a clever woman, our mother. She could have been, I don't know, a lawyer, a doctor, anything . . .' He paused.

'A bit more,' I said.

'It's so unfair,' he went on. '*I* had to work really hard, just to be average. While Luke passed every exam he ever took without doing a thing.' Jimmy shook his head. 'Life for Luke is just one big game,' he said. 'And now, of course, he's hit the jackpot!'

Deep in thought, Jimmy continued to cut my hair on the top until my parting disappeared, and it started to stand up.

'I wouldn't mind,' he said. 'But his fame and fortune are all thanks to me!' Jimmy picked up the mirror and showed me the back of my head. 'Well?' he said. 'Can I or can I not cut hair?'

'You can,' I said. 'But . . .'

He laughed. 'You'd like it a bit shorter.'

'At the back and sides,' I said.

Jimmy talked above the buzz of the clippers as he cut my hair very short. He explained how Lucky Luke had come to him and told him that he needed to look good for an audition. Apparently, he'd been out having dinner with his beautiful girlfriend when a TV producer had seen him. 'You could be perfect for a part we're casting,' the man said. 'Come for an audition tomorrow.' He had given Luke his card.

'This time,' said Jimmy, 'without even trying, Luke was about to get a top acting job. I was determined that for once he would fail. I gave him the worst haircut in the world.'

I laughed nervously. 'What was it like?' I said.

Jimmy switched off the clippers. 'Have you ever watched *Time Rider*?' he asked.

'You bet!' I said. 'It's brilliant.'

Time Rider was a new series on telly. It was about a joyrider called Bo, whose whole life is turned upside down when he drives off in a stolen time machine. Each episode was fast, exciting, and Bo himself was really funny. He was this tall, young bloke with . . . with the worst haircut in the world.

'Bo Danton's your brother!' I exclaimed.

'Also known as Luke MacDonald,' said Jimmy. 'Yes, that's him. Hard to believe, I know.'

I laughed. Jimmy had certainly had fun with his brother's hair. It looked as though it had been cut with a knife and fork. 'So he got the part despite the haircut,' I said.

'He got the part *because* of the haircut,' said Jimmy. 'The producer said that it looked "absolutely marvellous". He said it "reflected the inner chaos of the character". But did Luke thank me? Oh, no.' Jimmy shook his head. 'I'll never forgive him for what he did. Anyway,' he asked. 'Are you happy with your hair now?'

135   I examined myself in the mirrors. The haircut was fine. I could feel the breeze from the open window on my neck and ears. 'Nice and cool,' I said.

  'So you're going to pay, are you?' said Jimmy, as he brushed me down.

140   'Of course, I am,' I said.

  As he was searching for change in his nearly empty till, I asked the obvious question. 'What *did* he do?'

  Without looking up, Jimmy pointed at the newspaper. 'See for yourself,' he said.

145   I picked it up and began reading. The whole article was about Bo Danton's haircut. One sentence had been circled in blue ink. '*When asked about his hair, Luke laughed, "My brother's a barber. I think this is his idea of a trim."*'

  'You're the first person who's been here since then,' said
150 Jimmy. The newspaper was over a week old. 'And do you know the odd thing?' he said.

  I shook my head.

  'It should all be different. I thought people would come here to get a haircut, like the great Bo Danton. I could be
155 rich now. But it didn't work out like that. Some people are born lucky, and some people aren't,' he said, 'and there's nothing you can do about it.'

  As I was leaving, an old man and two boys passed me at the door. I turned to Jimmy. 'Maybe your luck's turning,'
160 I said.

  'I doubt it,' he said.

  Outside, the hot sun hit the back of my neck and the tips of my ears. I thought about Lucky Luke and realised that Jimmy was probably right. Unlike the weather, some things
165 in this world can't be changed.

Dining Out

Eva looked up from her menu, and stared at her aunt. As a girl, she remembered, Aunt Sophie had been too over-powering to be comfortable with. Eva was twenty-two now and they hadn't seen each other for over two years. When her aunt phoned and suggested lunch, Eva immediately felt that she was being summoned rather than invited.

Aunt Sophie caught Eva's eye and smiled. 'I've heard the red mullet is very good,' she said.

'It's also very expensive,' said Eva.

'Pffff!' she said, with a wave of her hand. 'Nothing is too expensive for my favourite niece.'

Eva shivered. With her hooked nose and long, sharp nails, Aunt Sophie had reminded Eva of a bird of prey. Now, after the two-year gap, she looked more dangerous than ever. Clearly, her aunt had heard about Eva's awful news, and had got back in touch to find out more. Eva was determined not to tell her anything.

'Red mullet would be lovely,' she said, and closed the menu. 'So, what have you been doing, Aunt Sophie?'

'Oh, this and that,' she said. 'Three months in Europe, ten weeks in the Far East.' Aunt Sophie worked for the Sydney Opera House, and her job involved a lot of travel-ling. 'And there's all the charity work at home . . . But what about you?' She stared into her niece's eyes. 'How are *you*, Eva, darling? You must tell your Auntie Sophie everything!'

★

By the time the bill came, Eva was feeling good. She had just eaten the best meal she'd had in a very long time, and, although her aunt asked her question after question, Eva had managed to keep her answers vague. Her private life had remained private.

If Aunt Sophie was irritated, she didn't show it. 'That was absolutely lovely,' she said, patting her napkin to her lips. 'We mustn't leave it so long again.'

'I know,' said Eva. 'I'm sorry, I . . .'

'Oh, my dear child,' Aunt Sophie interrupted. '*I'm* the one to blame. Always off, here, there and everywhere. From now on, I promise I'll try harder.'

Eva smiled. Perhaps, she thought, she'd got her aunt all wrong. Or perhaps, now that Eva was a woman, Aunt Sophie had decided to treat her as an equal. Whatever the reason, their meal *had* been fun. She'd forgotten how intelligent and witty her aunt was, and the stories she'd told about the people she met on her travels were hilarious. As they left the restaurant, Eva smiled again at the thought of all those people in such ridiculous situations. It was good to know that other people make fools of themselves, too.

'Now,' said Aunt Sophie. 'How are you going to get back?'

'No problem,' said Eva. 'There's a bus in ten minutes.'

'A bus!' said Aunt Sophie. 'Darling, I won't hear of it. *I'll* take you home.'

Eva knew it was pointless to argue. She followed her aunt to the car-park and guessed, at once, which was her car. It was the only sports-car there.

'Yes,' said Aunt Sophie, as they sped off in a cloud of dust. 'I still like to get from A to B as quickly as possible.'

'So I see,' Eva laughed.

Although she drove fast, Aunt Sophie had never had an accident. Her eagle-eyes never missed a thing. Eva sat back and enjoyed the ride – until she noticed the name on the sign which flashed past.

'Frankston!' she exclaimed. 'We're going the wrong way.'

Aunt Sophie turned and smiled. The sun glinted on her beak-like nose. 'I'm having such a lovely afternoon, darling,' she said. 'I just want it to go on for a little longer.'

'But where are we going?' said Eva.

'Your favourite place,' said Aunt Sophie. 'Phillip Island.'

As Eva walked along the boardwalks between the sand dunes, she realised her aunt was right. Phillip Island *was* her favourite.

When she was a girl, Eva had often come here with her parents. She'd always found Melbourne too big and noisy, and used to pretend that the island was her own special paradise. Now, every step Eva took brought back memories from that time, when life was simple and she was happy, unlike now.

She stopped, leant against the wooden balcony, and looked down at the beach as she had done countless times before. It was unfair of Aunt Sophie to bring her here, Eva thought. She didn't want to know how much her life had changed.

'You're crying, my darling,' Aunt Sophie said. Suddenly, it was all too much. Eva burst into tears and sank into her aunt's warm hug.

'But what is it?' asked Aunt Sophie softly. 'I thought you were doing so well. You've got your job, and the photography, and Andrew, of course . . .'

'He's gone,' said Eva. 'Andrew's left me. There,' she shouted angrily. 'That's what you wanted to know, isn't it?'

'My angel,' said her aunt, hugging her even more tightly.

'Believe me, I had no idea. Oh, you poor thing. I thought you were getting married.'

'So did I,' said Eva bitterly. 'So did the three hundred and fifty guests at the church. I can't remember where you were.'

'Rio,' said Aunt Sophie. 'But tell me more. When did you realise he wasn't going to turn up?'

Eva sniffed miserably. 'When the fax arrived,' she said.

'The fax!' Aunt Sophie exclaimed. 'He *faxed* you to say the wedding was off? You can't be serious!'

'I am!' said Eva. 'He sent it to the office . . .'

'The office!' Aunt Sophie cried. 'What on earth were you doing there on your wedding day?'

'I wasn't,' Eva said. 'But I haven't got a fax machine at home and . . .'

'So somebody else read it?'

Eva nodded. 'My boss,' she said. 'She rang me and read the fax out over the phone.'

'The worm!' Aunt Sophie exclaimed.

'She was very sympathetic,' said Eva.

'Not your boss,' she said. 'I'm talking about Andrew. He's a beast! And what did it say, this fax?'

Eva turned away and looked across at the sea. The first of the fairy penguins were arriving at the shore. They came every evening, full of food for their young, who lived in the cliffs at the other side of the beach.

Eva felt her aunt's heavy arm on her shoulder. 'Get it off your chest, Eva, darling,' Aunt Sophie whispered. 'I'm sure it'll make you feel better.'

Eva nodded. Talking about it did make her feel better. And, of course, she knew the fax off by heart. '*I cannot marry you,*' Eva said. '*I like you, perhaps I love you, but the thought of us spending the rest of our lives together fills me with terror. We are young. We need to grow. One day, I hope you will forgive me.*'

'Oh, Eva!' Aunt Sophie gasped. 'You're better off without him, believe me . . . Was that *all* he wrote?' she added.

'No,' said Eva. 'He said he'd be out of town for a month. He asked me to pick up any of my belongings from his apartment while he was away . . .'   135

'You're joking!' said Aunt Sophie, horrified.

'. . . and to post my key through the letter box when I'd finished,' Eva went on.

'Oh, you poor child,' her aunt said, and stroked her   140
hair. 'It must have been so awful for you to go back there.'

By now, Eva couldn't have stopped even if she'd wanted to. Lulled by her aunt's soft voice and fingers, Eva told her everything. She told her about the 10-kilo bag of cress seeds   145
that she had thrown all over the flat, except in the lounge, where she had taken more care, and how she had watered the whole lot for over an hour before leaving.

'Priceless!' Aunt Sophie exclaimed when Eva was finished. 'But what did you mean you took more care in   150
the lounge?'

'I . . . I spelt something out in big letters,' she explained. 'Right the way across the carpet.'

'What?' asked her aunt excitedly.

Eva smiled at the memory. 'We need to grow,' she said.   155

Aunt Sophie clapped her hands together. 'Marvellous!' she laughed. 'Eva, my darling, that is the best story I have heard in *ages*!'

Eva turned away again. In the half-light, she noticed one of the fairy penguins in the middle of the beach. A large   160
gull was attacking it. The gull couldn't do any real harm, but it tricked the penguin into thinking it was a bird of prey. Terrified, the penguin brought back the food it had caught for its young, and stood there watching as, with a loud squawk, the gull gobbled it all down.   165

Eva knew that she, too, had been tricked. She felt empty, and rather foolish. Aunt Sophie would be dining out on her story for weeks to come.

The Abyss

With Helen gone and the wind still howling along the coast, I headed inland and north. A farmer gave me a lift as far as Ye. It was dark when we arrived, and the farmer asked whether I needed a room for the night. 'My cousin, Javier Sanchez,' he said. 'He has a *hostal*. Very nice rooms.'

'Fine,' I replied. I really didn't care where I stayed.

We drove through the small town, and stopped outside a large, white single-storey building. It stood out against the black volcanic *malpais* like a lamp in the dark night. The entire Sanchez family came out to greet us. They welcomed me like a long lost friend, and though the guesthouse was not yet open for tourists, Javier insisted I use their spare room.

That evening, we sat round the table eating a thick meat and vegetable soup. Javier introduced his family. Isabel was his wife, Magdalena, his mother and Maria his oldest child. The boys were called Felippe and Jose. When I nodded hello to them, they smiled and pointed into their bowls. '*Puchero canario*,' they said. When I tried to repeat the words, they giggled, until their mother hissed at them to be quiet. '*Perdona*,' she said, turning to me.

I lifted my hands and smiled. 'It's okay,' I said. I wanted to tell them how kind they were, but I could not. My lack of languages had annoyed Helen throughout our trip. 'Michael,' I said, pointing to myself.

'Miguel!' Javier laughed. He turned and said something to Maria in Spanish, and I saw her face turn red. She was sixteen or so, still young enough to blush.

'My father apologises that he cannot speak English,' she said, looking up. 'He asked me to welcome you to Ye.'

'You speak English,' I said.

She nodded, and her father spoke to her again. 'My father asks what brings you to Lanzarote,' she said.

'Tell him it's a long story,' I said.

Maria laughed. 'We haven't got a television,' she said.

I smiled back, took a deep breath, and began. I told them how Helen and I had come to Europe from Canada for two months of culture, but how, after six weeks of art galleries and museums, the pair of us were exhausted. 'Of course,' I said, 'it was all amazing, and so *old*. The paintings, the sculptures, the buildings – we even slept in beds older than the state of Canada. But the travel was difficult, and the more tired we got, the more irritable we became.'

The weather hadn't helped either, I remembered. We soon discovered why the air-tickets had been so cheap for January and February. It snowed in Stockholm, Berlin and Prague, and rained everywhere else. When we woke to a fourth day of heavy rain in Venice, we stopped arguing just long enough to agree to spend our last fortnight in the Canary Islands.

The temperatures on Lanzarote were, as promised, up in the mid-twenties, it wasn't raining, and the Playa Blanca was as beautiful as it looked in the photos. But the brochure hadn't mentioned the wind. Howling in from the east, it turned the beach into a sandstorm, which stung our legs as we walked down to the sea, and made sunbathing impossible.

'This is *horrible*!' Helen shouted, and pulled away. I watched her disappearing into the swirling sand. Things were going from bad to worse. Everything about me annoyed Helen; the things I said, the things I did, the things I *didn't* do . . .

The next day, we took a coach to the Timanfaya National Park. All around us, the black lava stood up in jagged peaks like the surface of the moon. Nothing grew. I thought it was incredible, but kept my opinion to myself. I knew that whatever I said, Helen would disagree.

We walked towards the edge of the barren, smoking landscape. Helen turned to me and took both my hands in hers. I went to kiss her. She turned away.

'I'm sorry, Michael,' she said. 'It's over.'

As I finished my tale, I looked up to see that there were tears in Maria's eyes. Javier, too, was looking unhappy. He demanded to know what I had said and, as Maria translated, he stared at me fiercely. I thought I had somehow embarrassed the family by being so open. I had said too much – something else that had always annoyed Helen. When Maria and her father started arguing, I didn't know what to do.

Finally, Maria turned to me again. 'My father says he will take you on a trip tomorrow,' she said. 'He also says it is good that you chose to come here. In the ancient Guanche language of Lanzarote, Ye means "the end of the world".'

Javier was still staring at me. I smiled back, but my heart was pounding. Something odd was going on, something they weren't telling me about. I felt tired and anxious, out of my depth.

Although I went to bed that night determined to leave first thing the following morning, things did not work out as planned. Maria wasn't at breakfast, and when I told Javier I wanted to go, he misunderstood me. I was sitting in his four-wheel-drive when Maria appeared. She came running towards the car and stuck her head in my window.

'Remember,' she said. 'Whatever happens, my father is doing what he thinks is for the best.'

Before I had a chance to ask what *that* meant, Javier had set off. I felt more nervous than ever.

We drove on in silence past fields of cactus, the low sun bright in our eyes. After some while I realised we were following signs to Cueva de los Verdes.

I recognised the name from my guide book. Molten lava from a volcano had formed river, the outer edges cooled and hardened, while the centre continued to flow. It resulted in an underground cave system, some seven kilometres long. The book had also said that the *cueva* had lights, yet when we arrived, Javier gave me a torch.

He unlocked the door and the pair of us went down into the cool darkness underground. The lava was amazing, yellow, grey, orange, red; and the shapes! Where the river had turned to stone, it formed spiral pillars and dancing figures, as wonderful as any of the buildings and sculptures that Helen and I had seen.

We climbed stone steps, we crossed glistening chambers, we crawled through narrow tunnels, deeper and deeper into the earth. The further we went, the more uneasy I became. Despite the beauty of the cave, something about Javier's urgent behaviour frightened me. 'Where are we going?' I asked.

Javier turned and smiled. '*Que linda!*' he said, and kept walking. I had no choice but to follow him, along a narrow ledge, down some steps and across to the far end of a large chamber. There he stopped, turned and took me by the arms.

'Miguel,' he said. I was shaking so much, I couldn't reply. 'Miguel, I am sorry for you. With Helen.'

So he can speak a bit of English, I thought, and wondered how much of my story he had understood the previous night.

'You are sad,' he went on. 'You think it is like Ye, the end of the world.'

He turned and shone his torch ahead of him. I found myself staring at the most fantastic sight I had ever seen. High above my head, the cave looked like the inside of a great Gothic cathedral, below me, and just centimetres away from my feet, the ground opened up. I moved forward carefully and peered down into the abyss. I couldn't even see the bottom.   135

Suddenly, I felt hands on my shoulders. It was Javier. He was pushing me, pushing me over the edge. As I fell forward, I screamed and closed my eyes.   140

The next instant, I heard a splash. I stopped falling. My feet were wet, and I realised I was standing in a shallow pool of water. The abyss was just not real, just a reflection of the ceiling.

Javier was smiling. He reached down to help me out.   145
'*Not* the end of the world,' he said.

Mr Armitage

It was pure chance that Andy was looking at the local paper that particular afternoon. Normally he didn't bother, but the only other things to read in the dentist's waiting room were women's magazines and comics. The main story was about the demonstrations which had taken place against a planned new road. It was, however, a small article in the bottom right-hand corner that caught Andy's eye. HOMELESS EX-TEACHER DIES, the headline announced. Andy read on.

The body of Mr Sydney Armitage (68), of no fixed address, was discovered in bushes on the Newgate Estate yesterday. The cause of death was hypothermia. Mr Armitage taught maths at Raleigh Comprehensive School from 1969 until . . .

'Mr Reeves.' Andy looked up. 'If you'd like to follow me,' said the nurse. 'The dentist is ready to see you now.'

Although Andy hated dentists, the toothache had become so bad that he had to do something about it. As he followed the nurse to the surgery, however, Andy wasn't thinking about his tooth. For the first time in ages, it wasn't even hurting. He was thinking about Mr Armitage; the man who had shown him the difference between right and wrong.

★

Andy lay back in the chair with his mouth open and his eyes shut. He didn't want to see any of the sharp, shiny dentist's tools. He gripped the arms of the chair as the dentist set to work, and thought of Mr Armitage.

The maths teacher had always seemed strange to his 30
pupils. Throughout the autumn, he came to school every day with a freshly cut dahlia in his buttonhole. For the rest of the year, he wore a plastic one, or *ones*, for Mr Armitage had a wide selection. He always chose one which matched his tie and pocket handkerchief. 35

Mr Armitage was tall and very thin, and he had long white hair which he brushed back behind his ears. It looked like dove's wings. Andy couldn't remember the man ever shouting. When the class misbehaved, which was often, he would shake his head and whisper sadly, 'I bet Pythagoras 40
never had to put up with this.'

A teacher like Mr Armitage might have had a nickname, Beanpole or Pythagoras perhaps, or Dahlia, but he didn't make a big enough impression on the children for them to choose a special name. Mr Armitage he was, and Mr 45
Armitage he remained.

He had taught Andy for only one year. The boy's first year at the comprehensive school was Mr Armitage's last one. But Andy had met him again, three years later. He shuddered. The events of that Saturday afternoon still filled 50
him with shame.

'Okay,' said the dentist. 'If you'd like to rinse your mouth out.'

Andy opened his mouth and reached for the glass of pink liquid. He explored the hole in his tooth with his tongue. 55
It felt enormous. He spat into the basin, leant back in his chair and closed his eyes again.

It was the summer holidays, and Andy had just turned fourteen. He, Vinny, Dexter and Tel were over the derry, 60 an area of old buildings ready to be knocked down. This was where they spent most of their time. There was always something to do there, and no adults around to see them doing it!

65   That particular afternoon, Andy remembered, they had set fire to some old rags and papers with a magnifying glass. Vinny had found a silver thimble, Tel had cut his knee on a piece of rusty metal. They were on their way home when Dexter saw the tramp sitting in a broken doorway. He

70   turned to the others, and pointed. 'Bet he stinks,' he said.

'Oy!' yelled Vinny. 'When did you last have a bath?'

The tramp didn't say anything. Vinny marched towards him. 'I'm talking to you,' he said.

75   'Yeah, you dirty old dosser,' said Tel, following him. 'What are you doing here, anyway?'

Andy held back. He never liked it when Vinny and Tel got nasty, and the old man looked harmless enough.

'Why don't you clear off!' Vinny shouted, and he picked

80   up and threw a stone at him. It hit the door-frame and landed at the tramp's feet. Dexter and Tel cheered, and picked up stones of their own. The tramp retreated into his brown overcoat like a tortoise into its shell.

Andy watched in horror, as his three friends continued

85   to throw stones at the old man. He couldn't move, he couldn't speak. Suddenly Vinny turned round and stared at him angrily.

'What's the matter with you, then?' he said.

The others stopped and looked at him too.

90   'Nothing, I . . .' Andy began. Angrily, he bent down, picked up a small piece of broken brick and threw it as hard as he could. The stone spun through the air and hit the old man on his forehead. He looked up, as if surprised, and Andy saw the blood already pouring from the cut.

95   Slowly, the old man touched his forehead and inspected

his sticky, red fingers. He sighed, and whispered sadly, 'I bet Pythagoras never had to put up with this.'

'Right,' said the dentist. 'Bite down again. Fine. All finished.'

As Andy walked back to the reception, he remembered how, on that Saturday evening, he'd asked his mum what had happened to his old maths teacher. She'd told him that Mr Armitage had had a nervous breakdown after the death of his wife.

Later that night, Andy returned to the derry on his own. In his hand he was holding a twenty pound note, all his savings. He walked across the derelict ground to the doorway, but the old man was not there. 'Mr Armitage,' he called out. 'Mr Armitage, are you here? I've got something for you.' Andy's voice echoed away unanswered. Mr Armitage was gone.

Back at home, Andy slipped the money into his wallet. Four years later, he still hadn't spent it. He didn't feel it was his to spend.

The newspaper was still lying in the waiting room, and while the receptionist was writing down his next appointment in her book, Andy read the rest of the article. There was a burial service for Mr Armitage that afternoon at St Jude's. Andy looked at his watch. If he hurried, he should just get to the church in time.

'Is there a flower shop round here?' he asked.

'Yes,' said the receptionist. 'There's one almost opposite. You can't miss it.'

Despite the recent icy weather the shop was full of dahlias. 'They're grown in greenhouses,' the shop-keeper explained. 'Keeps the frost off them.'

Andy nodded sadly. Mr Armitage could have done with a greenhouse. He opened his wallet and unzipped the compartment at the back. 'I'd like some dahlias, please,' he said. 'Twenty poundsworth!'

'Any particular kind?' asked the woman.

Andy thought of the old man, but as his maths teacher, not as a tramp. He remembered the matching buttonhole, handkerchief and tie, and smiled. 'All sorts,' he said.

He thought Mr Armitage would like that.

The Final Memo

My next door neighbour, Mrs Brady, got me the job. She'd worked at Packer's Plastics for years, and when she heard I was looking for temporary work, she'd had a word with her boss, Mr Arnold.

The work wasn't that interesting. The company had just had a new computer system put in, and I had to transfer information from the old system to the new one. Still, there was a nice atmosphere in the office, everyone got on well.

There was Mrs Brady herself, who always shared her chocolate biscuits with me at morning coffee. She was Mr Arnold's secretary. There were three other computer operators, Jasmin, Carmen and Eric; old Ted, the caretaker, who wore grey overalls and was for ever checking his watch, Mr Patel, who worked in the post room, and his son Samir, who delivered and collected the mail – and then there was Trevor.

I saw him on my third day. He came up from the stockroom to put some cups into the coffee machine. 'Trevor Marchmont!' I said.

'Pete Carson!' he grinned. 'How's it going, mate?'

'Okay,' I said, and explained that I was going to college in September. 'That's why I'm working here,' I said. 'And you? How's the band doing?'

Trevor nodded. 'Okay,' he said. 'We had that single out,

5

10

15

20

25

33

and we play live most weeks.' He looked down. 'Working in this place pays the rent, know what I mean? Anyway,' he said, turning away, 'I'll see you around.'

I nodded, and watched as he disappeared through the swing doors. I'd been so jealous of Trevor Marchmont when I was sixteen. Trevor had left school so that his band could go professional. A year later, while I was in the middle of my A-levels, the Fins first single went to number 3. Since then, I hadn't heard much of them, and had sometimes wondered what happened to Trevor. Now I knew.

On the Wednesday of my fifth week at Packer's Plastics, Mr Arnold had a heart attack in the executive bathroom, and died. Mrs Brady couldn't stop crying, and between us we got through a whole packet of chocolate digestive biscuits.

A replacement was soon found, and on the following Monday there was a new name on the manager's door, *Nigella O. Snape*. The moment the woman herself burst into the office we all knew things were going to change.

Unlike Mr Arnold, Mrs Snape liked order. 'A place for everything and everything in its place', was her motto. That included us. She made it clear that she didn't like anyone leaving their desks, even during the breaks, and that she preferred her office to be quiet at all times. She communicated through memos, and insisted that we did the same. Overnight, the atmosphere had become cold and officious. On the following Tuesday things came to a head.

As she marched towards the door that morning, Mrs Snape noticed that the photocopier was running out of paper. She stopped and turned. 'Memo to stockroom, Mrs Brady,' she said. 'Fourteen packs of white copier bond paper. Thank you.' The next moment, she was gone.

'I don't know,' Mrs Brady grumbled to me. 'It's memos this and memos that . . . I wouldn't mind,' she went on, 'but it worked well enough before, *without* memos.' Just then, Samir arrived with the post. 'Thanks, lovey,' said Mrs Brady. As he was about to go, she added, 'Samir, could you get the stockroom to send up fourteen packs of white copier bond paper.'

'Yes, Mrs Brady,' said Samir.

Mrs Brady looked at me and winked. 'Just like the old days,' she said.

I smiled back. I had no idea my old neighbour was such a rebel. Sadly, her small act of defiance went very wrong.

Back in the post room, Samir passed the message on to his father. 'Forty packs of white copier bond paper,' he said.

Mr Patel, who was too busy to deal with the request himself, told Ted.

'Forty packs of wide copier bond paper,' he told him.

Ted was half way to the stockroom when he suddenly remembered something else he had to do. Mrs Tilly from the canteen was walking towards him.

'They need forty packs of wide floppy bond paper,' he explained to her.

Mrs Tilly passed the message onto Sam. 'Forty sacks of wide floppy bond paper,' she said. And it was Sam, who finally delivered the message to the stockroom.

'They want forty sacks of wide floppy bog paper up on the fourth floor,' he announced, and laughed. 'I hate to think why!'

Now Mr Grimble would have known immediately what the message should be. Mr Grimble knew everything there was to know about paper. Unfortunately, he and Mrs Grimble were lying on a beach in the Algarve. Trevor was standing in for him.

I didn't take much notice as Trevor wheeled his trolley through the office the first couple of times. Since our first meeting, we hadn't talked again. I think we both felt a bit awkward. When he walked past my desk for the eighth time, I had to ask what he was doing.

'Bog paper,' he replied, and laughed. 'It's come to this! But not for much longer,' he added. 'I've signed on at college. I'm going to do some exams.'

'That's great,' I said.

'Yeah, I start in October,' he explained.

At that moment, there was a crash and a scream from the far end of the room. We all jumped up and ran to see what had happened. The noise had come from the executive bathroom. Mrs Brady pushed the door open. We all gasped.

There was Mrs Snape lying on the floor under forty sacks of toilet paper. She wasn't moving.

'Do you think she's all right?' said Mrs Brady.

'Of course I'm not all right!' came Mrs Snape's furious voice. 'Get these things off me!'

Between us, it only took a couple of minutes to pile the sacks up again.

'What *are* they?' demanded Mrs Snape.

'Forty sacks of bog paper,' said Trevor. 'It's as wide and floppy as I could get.'

'Wide and floppy?' she said slowly. Suddenly, Mrs Snape realised what had happened. She turned on Mrs Brady. 'I thought I told you to send a memo,' she said.

'I . . . errm . . . that is . . .' said Mrs Brady nervously.

'That's what memos are for, to prevent this sort of thing,' she went on angrily. 'I need a secretary I can rely on, Mrs Brady. Do you understand me?'

I'd known Mrs Brady all my life. She had been like an extra grandmother when I was growing up. I certainly didn't like the way Mrs Snape was talking to her.

'It was me,' I said. Mrs Snape spun round. 'Mrs Brady gave me the memo,' I explained. 'But I'm afraid I lost it.'

Mrs Snape glared at me. I knew she didn't believe a word. 'In future,' she said, at last, '*all* communication will be done by memo. If you lose one, you get a new one. Is that clear?'

'Crystal clear, Mrs Snape,' I said. 135

The following morning, I got to work early. By the time the others arrived, I'd finished my own memos. I handed them out to Mrs Brady, Jasmin, Carmen and Eric.

Good Morning! they read.

Mrs Snape must have heard us laughing, but she stayed 140
in her office. When Samir turned up and I handed him his *Good Morning!* we all started laughing again. Then Carmen handed Samir her *Good Morning!*, and Samir in turn gave one of his to Eric – and so it went on. The office was in uproar. 145

Suddenly, Mrs Snape appeared. 'What do you all think you're doing?' she shouted. She snatched up a memo and read it. Then she turned to me. 'Are you responsible for this?' she asked. I nodded. 'I'll see you in my office, *now*,' she ordered, just as I had known she would. 150

I was ready for her, however. I stood up, unfolded my final memo and held it up for everyone to read. *It's okay*, it said. *I resign!*

Fireworks

'I wish we hadn't come,' David whispered to his wife.

David Grant hated fireworks. He knew how dangerous they could be.

Sarah Dawson's invitation had arrived three weeks earlier. At the time, the Firework Party seemed a long way off, but now it was already November 5th. Ten adults and fourteen children were out in the Dawsons' garden, waiting for the display to begin. David watched the older boys playing near the bonfire. His heart began to pound. He turned to his wife. 'I wish we hadn't . . .'

'I heard you the first time,' Miriam interrupted sharply.

'Well, I do,' said David. He felt miserable. Being there was bad enough, but Miriam's anger made it even worse.

'Why don't you go and check Sebastian?' she said finally.

David nodded. He thought of their five-month-old baby tucked up, warm and safe, in his cot in the spare bedroom upstairs. How he envied him! 'I won't be a minute,' he said.

Miriam shrugged. 'Take as long as you like,' she said.

The kitchen was hot, and smelled of the potatoes baking in the oven. David looked round. Bowls of salads and plates of meats and cheeses lined the worktop. Next to them were the glasses, all polished and waiting to be filled. Sarah

Dawson loved parties. The fireworks were just an excuse.

David found the baby alarm and held it to his ear. The sound of his son's gentle breathing calmed him. He smiled. 'There's a good boy, Sebastian,' he whispered. 'You stay asleep. You don't want the nasty fireworks to frighten you.' He put the baby alarm down and looked out through the window.

Dan Dawson was making sure that everything was safe. He checked the nails which fixed the Catherine Wheels to the fence posts; he checked that the Roman Candles would not fall over and that the rockets were all standing upright. David sighed. As far as he was concerned, the only safe firework was a dead firework. He saw Miriam swatting at something with her hand.

'A wasp!' he heard her exclaim. 'At *this* time of year!'

'I know!' Sarah replied, and laughed. 'I suppose that's the price we have to pay for such wonderful summers. We've decided to stay in England for our holiday next year,' she went on loudly. 'I mean, what is the point of going abroad, when it's so hot here?'

David had always thought that Sarah Dawson was a silly woman, now he knew it. Wasps in November, leaves still on the trees, the last five summers the hottest on record, and each one hotter than the year before. Something was seriously wrong. The climate was changing. The world was getting warmer, and all silly Sarah Dawson could think about were her summer holidays. David looked down at the baby alarm.

'Oh, Sebastian,' he whispered. 'What sort of world have we brought you into?'

If no one had come into the kitchen, David would have stayed there until the firework display ended. Unfortunately, someone did come. It was Kevin, Sarah and Dan's eldest boy. He'd been sent to check the potatoes.

'Hello, Mr Grant,' he said cheerfully. 'You'd better come out now. Dad's just about to start.'

David smiled awkwardly. It was nine months or so since he had last seen Kevin. In that time, the boy had grown into a tall and confident young man. He made David feel oddly childish. 'I . . . I was making sure Sebastian was all right,' he explained.

'He'll be fine,' said Kevin, and slammed the oven door shut. 'Come on,' he said. 'The fireworks won't look half as good from in here.' He held the door open.

David smiled again. He knew he had to go outside. 'Thanks,' he said, and followed Kevin back into the garden.

David walked across the lawn towards Miriam. He took hold of her hand and squeezed it.

'How was he?' she asked.

'Fine,' said David. 'I just hope the loud bangs don't wake him up.'

'Oh, for Heaven's sake, relax!' Miriam hissed.

Before David could protest, the first rocket of the evening shot up into the sky. It exploded in a shower of pink and green. Everyone, including Miriam, cheered. David looked at his wife, and wondered why she was being so unkind; why she didn't see how brave he was trying to be.

More rockets flew into the sky. Gold and silver, red, green and blue, they whistled and crackled far up above his head. The spectators went ooooh! and aaaah! as, one by one, the fireworks became more and more spectacular.

All at once, the air was filled with the deafening BANG! of a Cannon. Everyone screamed, then fell silent, and then started to laugh, nervous and embarrassed. Everyone, that is, except David Grant. He pulled away from Miriam and stood trembling, with his hands over his ears, and when the Roman Candles began pouring out their fountains of gold, he closed his eyes too. The acrid smoke blew towards him. It filled his mouth and nose. It filled his head with memories he wanted to forget.

David was thirteen, the same age as Kevin, when the accident happened. It was two days before Guy Fawkes' Night, and he and his best friend, Russell Tomkins, were in his dad's shed. That morning, they had bought a box of thirty small fireworks which they planned to turn into three really fantastic ones.

David cut the tubes open with his penknife and tipped the black powder into a bowl. Russell stirred it all up.

'I wonder what they called gunpowder when they first invented it?' he remembered Russell saying, as he spooned the mixture into the cardboard tubes. 'I mean, they didn't have guns then, did they?'

David also remembered his reply. 'Funpowder, I expect!' *Funpowder!* That was a laugh. How stupid I was then, he thought.

When they were finished, the three new fireworks looked great. 'Just like the real thing,' Russell had said. It was then that David noticed the box of matches in Russell's hand.

'What are you doing? NO!' he screamed – but it was already too late.

Russell had only meant to set light to the tiny amount of powder still remaining in the bowl. Unfortunately, this was not the only gunpowder in the shed. When he had stirred it all together, little bits had flown up into the air. As the match burst into flame, it was these bits which caught fire.

The first explosion blew off the door and sent Russell flying outside. David was not so lucky. One after the other after the other, the three homemade fireworks went off. He awoke, two days later, in hospital. He was lying on his front. His back, his hands and his left leg were badly burnt. The doctors all agreed he was lucky to be alive.

From that day on, David Grant was a changed person.

He became shy and awkward. He refused to do anything which meant taking his shirt off, gym, swimming, sun-bathing; and he wore cotton gloves to hide the scars on his hands. Adolescence came and went, but David was too frightened to get to know any girls. He was twenty-two before he had his first kiss, and that was with Miriam.

He had seen a film the week before, a film in which the heroine was also scarred. When her boyfriend had first seen the angry red marks on her shoulder he asked about them. 'Scars?' she'd said. 'What scars?' The boyfriend had smiled, and kissed them. The scars were never mentioned again.

So it was that when he bumped into Miriam in the Kool Kafé, and she had asked, over coffee and croissants, about *his* scars, he too had said, 'Scars? What scars?'

Miriam, however, had not seen the film. '*Those* scars!' she'd said. 'All over the back of your hands,' and she pulled down the white gloves to expose them.

David had smiled. It wasn't the reaction he expected, but it was honest and direct, and without the horror that he saw in other people's eyes. He leant forward, and kissed her. Three months later they were married.

David slowly removed his hands from his ears, and opened his eyes. He turned towards his wife, but she wasn't there. He heard the sound of a baby crying. 'Sebastian!' he cried.

As he ran past the kitchen door, David heard Miriam's voice coming from the baby alarm. 'There, there,' she was saying. 'Mummy's here now.'

He paused, and listened. His wife wasn't alone.

'The poor little lamb,' he heard Sarah saying. 'Your daddy doesn't like them either.' Her voice changed as she talked instead to Miriam. 'He looked absolutely terrified.'

'He had a bad accident when he was young . . . he . . .' She paused. 'I *hate* seeing him like that!' she said.

'Lucky it's only once a year,' Sarah laughed. 'Now if you lived in Spain! – they have fireworks all the time.'

'It's not just the fireworks,' said Miriam quietly. 'He's frightened of everything: water, animals, heights, driving, the future, the past . . . It's as if he never grew up, Sarah. 170 He's like a little boy.' She started crying. 'And now I've got Sebastian . . .' she said tearfully. 'I just can't cope with two of them.'

'Oh, Miriam,' said Sarah. 'I didn't realise . . . What are you going to do?' 175

Miriam sighed. 'I've had enough,' she said finally. She sounded calmer now. 'I'm leaving him.'

David closed his eyes. His legs felt weak, his scars hurt. Inside him, he heard a terrified boy's voice screaming, 'No!', and his head was filled with fireworks, dazzling and 180 deafening, exploding one after the other after the other.

The Shikara Man

When Auntie Meena – one of Jotinda's Punjabi relatives –
heard that he and Mark were spending the last week of
their Indian trip in Kashmir, she laughed. 'We Indians say
that Kashmiris like the truth so much, they don't like to
give it away,' she said. Her face became serious. 'You take
care up there.'

Mark remembered her words as he and Jotinda climbed
down from the bus in Srinagar. They were immediately
surrounded by a crowd of men and boys, all offering rooms.
Mark pushed through them. Joe, on the other hand,
stopped to talk.

'Typical!' said Mark irritably when he saw his friend
appearing from the crowd. He wasn't alone, and the man
with him was carrying Joe's backpack.

'This is Akbar,' he said. 'He's got a houseboat . . .'

'How much?' said Mark at once.

'Very reasonable,' said Akbar.

'How much?' Mark repeated.

'Top class and with best views of Dal Lake,' said
Akbar.

Mark stopped walking. '*How much*?'

'Twenty-six rupee,' said Akbar. 'Good price. No rats,
no cockroaches, no mouses.'

'Mice,' said Mark quietly.

'*Or* mice!' said Akbar.

44

Mark smiled. The price did sound reasonable. 'How do we get there?' he asked.

Akbar looked towards the lakeside and scratched his head. 'I have shikara,' he said, pointing to his boat. 'I'll ferry you across.'

'Okay, then,' said Mark at last. 'But if we don't like the houseboat, will you ferry us back?'

'You *will* like the houseboat,' said Akbar. 'I swear.'

Akbar was right. Mark and Joe did like the houseboat. They liked it so much that they paid for the full week.

Every morning, they got up early to watch the sun appear from behind the snow-capped Himalayas. Every evening, they sat in their deckchairs and watched it setting over the lake.

'This is the life,' Mark said.

'You can say that again,' said Joe.

'This is the life,' Mark repeated.

Their laughter echoed over the still water. It was their fifth evening on the houseboat.

'By the way,' said Mark. 'I was right. The houseboats *were* built by the British. Apparently, the local Maharajah refused to sell them any land. Instead, he let them live on the lake itself. The first one was built in 1888.'

'Is that so?' said Joe.

Mark smiled. He knew Joe wasn't interested. Mark was studying World Religions at university. For him, the trip to India was a chance to see all the things he knew only from books. Joe, on the other hand, was studying Computing. His parents were Indian, but Jotinda Talwar had been born in England. He was English. He knew nothing of India.

Mark looked across the water, and thought of Akbar. The shikara man did far more than ferrying. He'd organised day-trips. He'd helped them shop for bargains. He showed them the best restaurants when they wanted to eat out, and cooked for them on the houseboat when they didn't. In short, he was a real Jack of All Trades – or, as Joe put it, an Akbar of All Trades.

'What time is he picking us up tomorrow?' Mark asked.
65 He and Joe were planning to spend their last day cycling right round the lake.

'Half past seven,' said Joe.

'I hope he isn't late,' said Mark. 'The man at the Bike-Hire place told us to be there by eight.'

70 'He's been very good so far,' said Joe.

Mark nodded. Despite Auntie Meena's warnings and his own worries, he knew that Joe was right. Akbar *was* good.

Later on, as he lay in bed, Mark found himself thinking
75 about the shikara man again. When it was sunny, he was cheerful. When it clouded over, Akbar's mood also became darker.

Mark remembered their first crossing. The sun was shining and Akbar was talking non-stop, about Kashmir,
80 India, and his own life on the lake. 'Everybody knows Akbar,' he said. 'You need anything, anything at all, I can get it for you.' The sun glinted on his gold-toothed smile. His eyes narrowed. 'How many children have you got?' he asked.

85 'None,' they both replied.

Akbar smiled again. 'Kashmiri men are strong,' he said, and scratched absent-mindedly at his thick, wavy hair. 'I have four children. Three daughters, and a son,' he said proudly. 'His name is Akbar, like me. We live on a boat
90 over there,' he said, nodding into the distance.

'How old is he?' asked Joe politely. 'Your son?'

'Six,' said Akbar. 'But one day, he will also be a strong Kashmiri man,' he laughed. 'Like me.'

It was on a dark and stormy afternoon that Mark first
95 saw Akbar's darker, stormier side. Mark and Joe were going

46

to a cafe which their guide book recommended. Akbar was not happy.

'Stupid guide books,' he muttered. 'Make one man rich while others go hungry. You put cafe in the guide book and all the sheep come running! Baaah! Baaah!' he shouted. 'BAAAAH!'

Suddenly Mark sat up in bed. He'd been dreaming. Outside he could hear the sounds of splashing water and screaming voices. He ran out onto the deck. Joe was already there.

'What's going on?' he said.

'No idea,' said Joe. He pointed to a boat about fifty metres away. In the light of the flashing torches and flickering oil lamps, they could see men jumping into the lake and splashing about in the water. On the deck, the women were still screaming. 'Waaah! Waaah!' they screamed. 'WAAAAH!'

Mark and Joe watched for a bit more, but there was nothing they could do. They went back to their beds. Mark wrapped the pillow round his head. He had no more dreams that night.

Another shikara man came at half past seven, but Mark and Joe sent him away. Akbar, however, didn't appear all morning, and they finally got a boat at one o'clock. By then, of course, the bikes were all gone. Mark and Joe went instead to a cafe for lunch. There, they got talking to an Australian woman about the disturbance on the lake the previous night.

'It was a boy,' she told them. 'A six-year-old boy. Apparently, he was walking in his sleep, and fell off the boat. His feet got tangled up in the weeds and . . . oh, it's so awful!'

Mark and Joe looked at one another. They knew that Akbar lived on the lake. They knew he had a six-year-old son.

'Come on,' said Joe. 'Let's see if we can find him.'

Clouds were rolling in from the north when they arrived at the lakeside. The water was dark, and getting rough. They went to the place where Akbar kept his shikara, and
135 there was the man himself, looking out across the water. Mark and Joe stopped and stared.

'He's shaved his head!' Joe exclaimed.

'He's in mourning,' said Mark quietly. 'The women wear black. The men shave their heads.'

140 'So it *was* his child,' said Joe.

At that moment, Akbar turned. He saw Mark and Joe staring at him. 'Why are you not out on bicycles?' he said.

'We couldn't get a shikara,' Mark explained.

'But I told my uncle,' he said. 'Did he not come?'

145 Mark and Joe realised that this was the man they had sent away. As Joe explained, Akbar shook his head sadly. 'I had . . . other business,' he said.

'We know,' said Mark quietly. 'We understand.'

To his surprise, Akbar grew angry. 'No,' he shouted.
150 'You do not understand. You cannot understand.'

'I know. I mean, I'm sorry,' said Mark. 'I . . . I don't know what to say.'

'Then better say nothing,' said Akbar gruffly.

155 The three of them sat in the shikara in awkward silence as Akbar ferried them back towards the houseboat. They were half way there when the sun came out. Akbar looked round. 'Today is your last day,' he said. 'You still have not visited the other side of the lake. I . . . I am sorry about the
160 bicycles.'

Mark and Joe again assured him that it didn't matter, and were surprised when Akbar suggested that *he* ferry them across.

'Haven't you got . . . things to do?' Mark asked.

165 Akbar shrugged. The sun gleamed on his shaven head

48

as he turned towards the passing houseboats, and waved. From one of them, four grinning children waved back. There were three girls and one boy and, when Akbar shouted something out to them, the boy nodded and disappeared down inside the boat. 170

'He has gone to tell his mother that I will be late for supper,' Akbar laughed.

'That was your son, then?' said Mark. 'Little Akbar.'

The shikara man nodded proudly.

'But . . .' said Joe. 175

'The boy who died,' Mark interrupted. 'Did you know him?'

The shikara man looked from Joe to Mark, and back again. He frowned. 'Not well,' he said. 'Why?'

'I . . . that is, we . . . We thought . . .' Mark said. 180

'Akbar,' said Joe. 'You've had your hair cut and . . .'

Akbar rubbed his head with his hand and smiled. 'Ah, yes, this morning. Very nice, very cool – you like it?'

'It looks fine,' Mark said. 'We just wondered . . . why?'

For a moment, Akbar looked thoughtful. Then, his face 185 broke into a grin. 'Louses!' he said cheerfully, and the bright sun sparkled on his gold teeth. 'Always scratching. Now, no hair, no louses.'

'Lice,' said Mark with a grin.

'*Or* lice!' said the shikara man. 190

'Patata'

'Look, papa – peaches!' Savati cried out.

'They're enormous!' said Haresh. 'Can we have some? Can we, Papa?'

Shanti smiled. 'I don't see why not,' he said. 'I have heard that Italian peaches are almost as delicious as our Indian mangoes.' He pulled over to the kerb, and stopped the car just past the greengrocer's. 'Let us see for ourselves.'

Dr Shanti Vihar and his wife Chandra were on holiday in Europe with their three children, Haresh, who was nine, Savati, who was seven and Sunil, who would be four in August. Chandra's sister, Rupa, was married to an Austrian called Koenig. He, too, was a doctor. It was a family joke that the four Kothari sisters refused to marry a man from any other profession.

Chandra and Rupa had last seen each other five years earlier. As children, they were close and, with the help of the telephone, they tried to stay close as adults, but as Rupa so often said, 'Vienna and Bombay are a long way apart.'

At last, however, they were going to meet up again. Shanti had put a little money aside every month, and after three years he had enough for a trip to Europe. He found a cheap flight to Rome. 'We can hire a car with the money we save,' he told his wife. Together, they planned their route. Rome to Florence, Florence to Venice, then possibly north to Munich, and on to Vienna. They were as excited as two small children.

Before they left Bombay, Chandra went into the city to buy a couple of things for Rupa and her family. As usual, she went mad! She bought books and CDs, jewellery and saris, heavy with gold and silver thread, glasses and bowls, spices and incense, a vase she just knew Rupa would love – and a dozen videos of the latest 'Bollywood' movies.

At the airport, Shanti discovered they were carrying twice their baggage allowance. He was not amused. 'But I don't understand you, Shanti-ji,' Chandra said. 'My Rupa is worth every extra rupee.'

As they entered the greengrocer's, Shanti breathed in the smell of strawberries and ripe melons. He turned to his wife. 'Not like old Faroukh's,' he said.

Chandra laughed. She knew what Shanti meant. Their neighbour's so-called Fruit 'n Veg Emporium always smelt of rotting straw. She looked round at the display of fruit and vegetables, all neatly laid out on wooden trays, and sighed. 'Bombay is such a dirty city,' she thought.

When the shop-keeper appeared, it was immediately clear that he could not speak English, let alone Hindi. Chandra knew a little German and French, but this was the first time she had heard Italian. She thought it sounded like running water. Using their fingers to point and to count, Chandra and the shop-keeper managed to communicate.

The fruit and vegetables were all labelled with their names: *arance*, *fragole*, *melanzane*, *patate*, and Savati and Haresh were repeating them out loud. When he realised what they were doing, the shop-keeper burst out laughing.

'*Che carino! Che carina!*' he said. '*Questi bambini!*'

Chandra smiled proudly. 'Savati,' she said, pointing to her daughter. 'Haresh, and Sunil.'

'Savati, Haresh and Sunil,' the shop-keeper repeated. He pointed to himself. 'Antonio,' he said, and walked over to the children. '*A-ran-ce*,' he said slowly, and pointed to the sign in the oranges. The children repeated the word. He turned to the strawberries. '*Fra-go-le*,' he said. Again, the children repeated the word exactly. Haresh reached forwards and picked up a potato.

'*Pa-ta-te!*' he announced.

Antonio shook his head. He pointed to all the potatoes in the tray. '*Pata-TE*,' he said. '*Pata-TA*,' he added, touching Haresh's single potato.

'*Patate* must be the plural,' said Savati.

'I *know* that!' Haresh shouted back. His sister was such a know-all!

Antonio threw his head back and roared with laughter. '*Sono incantevoli*!' he said, turning back to Chandra.

Although she smiled, Chandra was annoyed. The children were getting far too excited. 'Six . . . *pesche*, please,' she said, pointing to the peaches and raising six fingers. 'Children, do be quiet! Shanti, *do* something!'

Friends once more, Haresh and Savati were now marching round the shop, with Sunil following them. All three were shouting at the tops of their voices, 'Pa-ta-ta! Pa-ta-ta! Pa-ta-ta!'

'I'm ashamed of you,' Chandra said angrily. They were all back inside the car. 'You are abroad now, and must behave – or do you want everyone to think that Indian children have no manners?'

'But he liked us, mama,' said Haresh.

'That's enough!' Chandra shouted. 'I don't want to hear another word.' She turned to her husband. 'Shanti, are we going to sit here all day?' she said impatiently.

Shanti turned the key in the ignition for the fourth time. The engine gave a little cough, but did not start. He shook

his head. 'Something's wrong,' he said and got out of the
car.

As he stared down at the engine, Shanti wished that he
understood about cars. Sadly, he knew it was a wish that
would never come true. 'I'll have to call a garage,' he called   100
to his wife. 'Perhaps Antonio will let me use his phone.'

Chandra nodded. 'That's the problem with doctors,' she
thought irritably. 'They are useless with anything practical.'
Rupa was always saying the same about *her* husband.

Just then, a scooter with two young men on it pulled up   105
next to Shanti. 'You speak English?' the man on the back
asked.

'Yes,' said Shanti, surprised. 'Yes, I do . . .'

'And you have a problem?' he asked.

'The car won't start,' Shanti said. 'I'm not sure . . .'   110

'I look,' said the man. 'Perhaps I can help. I am Marco.
This is Giorgio.'

Inside the car, Chandra smiled. 'What a friendly place,'
she thought. 'In Bombay, everyone is always in such a rush.'

Marco climbed off the scooter, joined Shanti at the front   115
of the car and began working on the engine. 'Perhaps it
is your . . . *alternatore*. I don't know the English.' Shanti
shrugged. Neither did he. 'Perhaps it will take a long time,'
Marco added. 'It is hot in the car. Your wife and
children . . .' He pointed to the shadow on the pavement.   120
'Cooler for them.'

'Of course,' said Shanti. 'Chandra, children; why don't
you wait outside the car?'

As they climbed out, Giorgio rode off on his scooter. 'Is
okay,' Marco explained. 'He will come back. Now,' he said.   125
'Perhaps now we can try again.'

He closed the bonnet and climbed into the driver's seat.
Chandra watched him gratefully. They were so lucky to
find such a helpful young man. She turned to Haresh. 'I
hope you, too, will grow up to be so practical and . . .'   130

'Patata!' Sunil suddenly shouted out.

'Sunil, be quiet,' Chandra said. 'I have told you . . .'

'But mama, it *is* a patata!' he said. 'Look!'

135 What happened next, happened so quickly that Chandra could not stand and stare. First, she saw the potato. It was stuck onto the end of the exhaust pipe. Next, Giorgio returned. He sped towards the back of the car, braked hard, bent down, removed the potato and rode off in a cloud of
140 dust. Next Marco tried the engine. It started, of course, first time, and he too sped away.

'Well done!' Shanti cried. He turned to his wife. 'He did it,' he said.

Chandra stared at her husband. 'Shanti, you fool!' she
145 said. 'Don't you see what has happened? There was nothing wrong with the car. It was all a trick!' she shouted.

Chandra was angry. She was angry with Shanti, angry with Marco and Giorgio, angry with herself. In Bombay, she would not have fallen for such a trick. Here, on holiday,
150 she had forgotten that in every city in the world there are good people and bad people.

Shanti still didn't understand. 'A trick?' he repeated slowly.

Chandra explained.

155 'But . . . but . . .'

'They have robbed us,' said Chandra simply. 'Our clothes, my jewels – the presents for dear Rupa and her family: they have taken everything.'

Chandra stared at her husband. She was waiting for him
160 to start shouting and screaming. To her surprise, Shanti did neither. Instead, as Chandra looked on in horror, he roared with laughter, and began marching up and down the pavement.

'Pa-ta-ta!' he yelled. 'Pa-ta-ta! Pa-ta-ta! Pa-ta-ta!'

Origami

When he applied for the teaching job in Colombo, John knew that the school was offering only a local wage. They gave him accommodation, though, and he had hoped the money would be enough for him to live on.

So long as he did nothing in the evenings and weekends, it *was* enough – but John had not travelled to Sri Lanka to spend all his free-time locked up in the tiny flat. When he first arrived, he visited some of the island's places of interest: the ancient ruins of Anaradapura, the Kandy parade with its painted elephants and fire-eaters, the tea-plantations of Nuwara Eliya ... Now he wanted more.

There was, however, a problem. To see everything he wanted, he needed to earn more money – lots more!

Zoe, who also worked at the school, told him the going-rate for private lessons was 1,000 rupees an hour. It seemed a crazy amount, but then John knew that most of the Japanese and Europeans working in the country earned up to fifty times as much as he did. As Zoe put it, for them, the 1,000 rupees was a bargain. For John Merson it was a month's salary.

He placed an advertisement in the *Daily Observer*, and six days later received a reply from a Japanese couple: a Mr and Mrs Sato. He phoned their number at once, discovered that they wanted conversation lessons – one a week for ten weeks – and fixed a time for the lessons to take place. Things were going well. Then John spoke about the money. Mr Sato did not reply. Instead, John heard a sharp intake of breath.

30   'That's for the two of you,' he explained. He was beginning to think that Zoe had got it all wrong. 'One thousand per session.' For a second time, Mr Sato seemed to gasp. 'Is . . . is that okay?' John asked.

'Is okay,' came the abrupt reply.

35   John shook his head sadly as he put down the phone. Mr Sato obviously thought the lessons were too expensive, but was too polite to say. john didn't think the couple would turn up. It was therefore a surprise when, at seven o'clock on the dot, there was a soft knock at the door. John ran to open it.

40   'Mr and Mrs Sato,' he said. 'Do come in.'

That first lesson was difficult. Although they both got high marks in their written tests, Yajima and Yuko Sato found speaking extremely difficult. John knew that a large part of his work would be to build up their confidence. 'Where did you first learn English?' he asked.

45

'Aah . . . aah . . .' Mr Sato began. 'I . . . I . . . I learned English . . . I learned in the school.'

'At school,' John said, encouragingly. But Mr Sato had noticed the correction.

50

'Yajima! Yajima!' he growled. Then, all of a sudden, he began beating his forehead with the palm of his hand.

Mrs Sato stared down at the table.

'*At* school, *at* school, *at* school,' Mr Sato repeated, over and over again.

55

John watched in horror. He decided to make a note of any errors, so that they could look at them together more carefully – and less painfully – later in the lesson.

At eight o'clock, John sat back in his chair. The Satos closed their exercise books, and waited.

60

'Excellent,' said John, getting up. The Satos picked up their books, and stood behind their chairs. John handed them both some homework, and asked them to prepare a talk for the next lesson. 'About a Japanese saying,' he explained. 'A saying which will help me understand Japan.' 65

Mr Sato nodded. 'Is okay,' he said.

As he closed the door behind them, John remembered the money. 'Never mind,' he thought. 'It can wait.'

Back in his room he saw that the Satos had left him something after all. There on the table stood a crane, made 70
from a single sheet of blue paper. John placed it on the window sill and thought no more about it.

The second lesson went much better. The Satos again arrived at exactly seven o'clock. There were no mistakes in 75
their homework, and they were both obviously eager to start talking.

'We . . . aaah . . . have chosen . . . aaah . . . following saying,' Mr Sato announced. 'Nail that stands up is hammered down!' 80

Mrs Sato smiled and nodded. 'Which means, Japanese person must not be different. Must . . . aaah . . . must . . .'

'Confirm,' said Mr Sato, smiling and nodding.

'Conform,' said John, and immediately regretted it.

'Con*form*, con*form*, con*form*,' Mr Sato repeated, beating 85
his forehead over and over. Suddenly he stopped and looked up. 'Con*form*,' he said, and smiled.

As they talked, John noticed that Mr and Mrs Sato never once looked at each other. Their attention was fixed on him, their teacher. When he told them how well they were 90
speaking, they both looked down at the table and blushed.

Again, the matter of money did not come up. Again, John returned to the sitting room to find a small origami animal standing on the table.

This time, it was a yellow horse. He picked it up and 95

turned it over in his hand. Every fold had been done so carefully. It must have taken ages to make. Puzzled, John shook his head. 'I suppose they'll pay the whole lot at the end of the ten weeks.'

100   He placed the horse next to the crane.

The third lesson was actually fun. John had asked the Satos to prepare a Japanese joke and, for the first time, both of them seemed at their ease. They spoke more fluently than
105   before, and Mr Sato managed not to hit himself even once. 'This joke,' he explained, 'is one of many "What to do with Grandma" jokes.'

'I don't like them,' Mrs Sato interrupted, staring ahead.

'But many do,' said Mr Sato. He cleared his throat. 'If
110   you have a Grandma with a sweet tooth, then spread honey all over your . . . aaah . . . crockery. When she has finished licking it all off, the . . . crockery . . . will shine like new.'

John grinned. He liked black humour – and he enjoyed the discussion they had about the problems of an ageing
115   population.

A dragon joined the horse and crane on the window sill.

So it went on. Every week, the Satos would come for their lesson. Every week, John would find a new origami figure
120   to add to his collection.

At the end of the seventh lesson, however, things were a little different. Mr Sato cleared his throat, bowed and held out a present. 'Happy Birthday,' he said, looking down.

'And many happy returns,' said Mrs Sato.

125   John smiled awkwardly. He found himself bowing. 'Thank you,' he said. 'But how did you know?'

Mrs Sato smiled.

'You mentioned it in . . . aah, lesson four,' said Mr Sato.

'You are an Aquarius,' Mrs Sato added.

130   'Oh, yes!' said John. They were right. Somehow, that

evening, the discussion had turned to fortune-telling. Mrs Sato had confessed to using the I-Ching. Mr Sato, John remembered, had said hardly anything at all.

Later, when they had gone, John looked at the present. The wrapping alone was a work of art. The expensive paper had been neatly folded, tied up with ribbons and decorated with bows. It seemed a shame to open it. John didn't like to think of himself as greedy, but he started to imagine what could be inside the wonderfully wrapped gift. A personal stereo, perhaps, or a miniature television – something Japanese.

Beneath the paper, was a small wooden box. John placed it on the table, and removed the lid. Inside were six pairs of ornately decorated chopsticks. John smiled.

'Something Japanese!' he said.

With the final lesson over, John knew he would miss his weekly lessons with the Satos. They, it seemed, felt the same.

'We Japanese are an insular people,' Mrs Sato said.

'Surveys show that we have little interest in mixing with foreigners,' Mr Sato explained. 'It is shame . . . *a* shame,' he laughed.

'You are a good teacher, Mr Merson,' said Mrs Sato.

'It has been our pleasure to study with you,' Mr Sato added and, with a bow, he handed John his card. 'Please do . . . stay in touch,' he said.

As they left, Mrs Sato slipped something into John's hand. 'Thank you,' she said, and lowered her head. 'Thank you.'

John shut the door, and looked down. He was holding yet another folded piece of paper. This time it was a square wallet which had some banknotes inside. John counted them quickly. 'But there's only five thousand,' he said. 'It should be ten!'

He felt angry. Why had they cheated him? Why? They were friendly, they gave him their address. Didn't they think he would write to ask for the rest? It made no sense.

170 And then he noticed them; the row of origami figures on the window ledge. What was it Mrs Sato had once said? 'We Japanese do not like to show money.'

He picked up the blue crane and carefully unfolded it. Inside were two rolled 500 rupee notes. There was more inside both the yellow horse and red dragon. The white
175 swan he had received in the fourth week was different though. It contained *two* thousand rupees – and so did all the remaining figures.

All together, the Satos had paid him 20,000 rupees for their lessons. That made one thousand an hour, each – the
180 going-rate! John smiled, Zoe had been right after all.

Now he could explore every inch of the island.

Memory Lane

Miriam was finishing the washing-up when she heard the letter drop onto the mat. She dried her hands and went through to the hall. 'It's probably just a bill,' she thought.

It was not, however, a bill. It was a letter, an airmail letter – an exotic letter. Recently, the most exotic thing in Miriam's life was a tin of lychees she had for dessert two nights earlier.

'Who do I know in Singapore?' she said, as she held the thin, blue envelope. Miriam opened it, and went straight to the end of the letter. It was signed, *Yours, an old acquaintance*. There was no name.

Miriam turned the paper over and began at the beginning.

Kam Leng Hotel
Singapore 0820

Dear Miriam Gooch,
I don't remember you, but I hope that you may remember me.

Miriam paused. In all her forty-four years, she had never read a letter that started so strangely. 'You may not remember me, but . . .' – lots of letters began like that, but this was different. She read the sentence again. 'If you don't remember me, how do you know my name?' she wondered. Puzzled, Miriam read on.

About a month ago, I was attacked by muggers, and hit on the

61

head. I remember none of it. When I came round I found that I had lost not only my possessions, but also my memory. Amnesia isn't an illness, and so the hospital sent me home. I am now trying to discover who I am.

30   'A loony!' Miriam muttered to herself. Nevertheless, she could not stop reading.

Luckily, I have something to help me: my address book. It was in the back pocket of my jeans at the time of the mugging, and
35   was not stolen. It's very interesting. For a start, there is a name on the front page without an address. I am hoping that this is *my* name. Chris Lawrence. Do you remember anyone with that name?

Secondly, although – so I understand – most people list names
40   alphabetically, all the names in *my* address book are listed by places. Amritsar, Boston, Colombo, Copenhagen etc . . . I assume from this that I have spent much of my life travelling. Perhaps I used to find it easier to remember a face if I could remember where I first saw it. Your name appears under L, for
45   Leh. I have discovered that this is the capital of Ladakh, high up on the Tibetan Plateau in the north-east of India.

Miriam let her arm hang limply by her side. The pale blue paper rustled. 'Leh,' she whispered. 'It must be twenty years . . .' She went into the sitting room and sat down.
50   'Twenty-*two* years,' she said. 'Half my life ago.'

She realised that it was chance that this Chris Lawrence person had written to the correct name and address. After all, she'd been O'Donnell for seventeen of those twenty-two years. She changed her name back to Gooch after the
55   divorce. As for the address, she'd gone back to live with her mother after the divorce and hadn't managed to sell the house after her death.

'Leh,' she repeated bitterly. That was where it all started. As she continued reading the letter, icy shivers tingled up
60   and down her spine.

The other names listed under *Leh* are Rachel Taverner, Mark
Green, Lara Ichinaya and 'someone' O'Donnell. It could be
either Iain or Liam – I'm afraid I can't read my own writing.

Miriam pursed her lips. 'It's Iain,' she said, and scowled.   65
Even after five years, the pain of Iain's sudden departure
still hurt. He had been so cruel.

Of course, he wasn't always like that. Once, they were
in love; once, they were happy. But for Miriam, Iain's final
betrayal had wiped away all those years spent together. It   70
was as if they had never happened. Now, because of this
stupid letter, all her memories were coming back.

She did remember Rachel, and Mark. They were both
from Manchester. She was a nurse; he was trying to get
'into television'. And Lara was from New Zealand. Miriam   75
recalled that she had beautiful black hair. The four of them
– five, with Iain – were all staying at the Shalima, a simple
but clean guest-house close to the centre of town.

As travellers so often do, they got on well with one
another immediately. That first evening, they ate together   80
at a cafe called the Dreamland, and as the days passed,
more often than not, they went round as a group. They
explored the dusty markets, walked in the barren hills and
visited the Buddhist monasteries, or *gompas*. Apart from
Rachel and Mark, who were a couple, they were all travel-   85
ling alone. The company, Miriam remembered, made a
very welcome change.

She looked back down at the letter. 'The thing is,' she
said impatiently, 'I don't remember *you*!'

. . . in case you still don't remember, *she read*, I will describe   90
myself. I am 5 foot 10 inches tall and weigh 150 pounds. I've got
brown hair and greeny-brown eyes; nothing unusual I'm afraid,
apart from a tattoo of a rose on my left shoulder! One last thing:
under yours and Iain/Liam's name is a word I can't quite make
out. It looks like 'Spitok' . . .   95

'My God!' Miriam gasped. 'Spitok.'

It was the name of one of the *gompas*. From Leh, it was a bus-ride and a long uphill walk away. Miriam was sure that only she and Iain had gone there. If anyone else *had* been there, then her memory had chosen not to remember him. She shrugged. Certainly, a lot had happened on that day at Spitok Gompa.

She remembered the weather, burning hot one moment and freezing cold the next, and how the high altitude made her head spin and her heart pound. Boom boom boom, it went, just as it was pounding now.

She remembered seeing the *gompa* for the first time, and the monks in their maroon robes. She remembered the huge statue of the Buddha, the walls painted with screaming monsters, and the room filled with the dead birds hanging from the ceiling. Iain had asked the monk there what they represented. The monk, who couldn't speak English, took them to the Abbot.

Miriam closed her eyes. She could hear the Abbot speaking in that curious East-meets-West accent. '. . . The cycle of birth and rebirth . . . What goes around, comes around . . . Joy and sorrow: these too will change – until we let go . . .' She remembered that their meeting came to an abrupt end when the Abbot's digital watch, a present from a younger brother who worked on Wall Street, began peep-peeping. 'Dinner,' the Abbot announced happily.

Miriam and Iain ate with the monks; rice and curry, and a dark soupy drink in wooden mugs. Apparently, it was tea mixed with salty butter. It smelt so sour that Miriam was unable to drink hers, and asked for a glass of water instead. Although Iain didn't like the buttery tea either, he drank not only his own, but hers as well. He didn't want the monks to take offence.

It was, Miriam had thought, such a selfless thing to do, that she had fallen in love with Iain O'Donnell there and then. Six months later, and back in England, they got married. Everyone said they made a perfect couple.

Miriam sniffed. She wanted to stop remembering now, but it was impossible. The memories would not go away. She wiped away a tear and looked down angrily at the letter. 135 'Why did you have to write to me?'

After ten years of marriage, she and Iain decided it was time to start a family. She was thirty-two, he was thirty-four. They tried everything, but it was no good. Hospital tests confirmed that Miriam would never have children. Tiny 140 organisms in the water at Spitok Gompa, the only unboiled water she drank on the whole year-long trip, were the reason.

'And so he left me,' Miriam sighed bitterly. 'For someone younger and prettier – and fertile.' 145

I do hope that this letter finds you well. I look forward to hearing from you and pray that you will be able to fill in some of the gaps in my life.

'You stupid man!' Miriam shouted, and screwed the letter 150 up into a ball. 'If *you* can't remember who you are, why should anyone else?'

Glossary and Language Practice

Pluto

GLOSSARY

lace-up boots (line 9): 'laces' are like long pieces of string for tying up boots and shoes.

high heels (line 12–13): shoes with high heels for women.

her head in the clouds (line 13): someone who is a dreamer, and doesn't think about the ordinary things of life.

feet firmly on the ground (line 14): someone who is usually unimaginative and thinks about ordinary, everyday things.

a short-cut (line 16): a quicker way of getting somewhere than the usual route.

creepy (line 18): frightening, horrifying.

bungalows (line 19–20): one-storey houses.

net-curtain (line 25): a piece of very thin material hung at the window to prevent people from seeing in.

nosey (line 26): to interfere in other people's lives or business.

cloakroom (line 33): the place in a public building where you can leave your coat, umbrella, bag.

a blast of (line 37): a sudden powerful movement.

stand out (line 46): protrude, be noticeable.

giggly (line 48): to laugh in a childish way because you are amused or nervous.

The trouble is (line 51): if you start a sentence with 'the trouble is' you go on to describe a problem.

At least (line 58): you can use 'at least' to show that you are correcting what you have just said.

tissues (line 64): thin, soft pieces of paper that you can use as handkerchiefs.

dabbing (line 66): to touch something several times with quick, light movements, often to dry up a liquid.

a humpback whale (line 74): a large whale with a hump on its back and long flippers.

by the way (line 77): used in conversation when you want to introduce a new or different subject.

nickname (line 91): an informal name, usually taken from how somebody looks, or their real name.

ban (line 92): official ruling that something may not be done.

dolphin-friendly tuna fishing (line 92–3): tuna fishing which does not kill dolphins.

ivory (line 93): an expensive material made from elephant tusks.

global warming (line 94): the problem of the earth's temperature getting warmer and warmer.

vegetarians (line 95): people who choose not to eat meat or fish.

single (line 95): unmarried.

Gemini (line 96): a person whose sign of the zodiac is Gemini is born between mid-May and mid-June.

Aquarian (line 96): a person whose sign of the zodiac is Aquarius, is born between mid-January and mid-February.

a crank (line 99): someone who has strange ideas or beliefs.

passers-by (line 104): people who walk past.

before Emma explodes (line 122): (here) to express strong feelings, sometimes violently.

as ever (line 133): as usual.

for the umpteenth time (line 141): something that has happened a lot of times already.

stout (line 143): rather fat.

in a thick bun (line 144): the hair is up, twisted round into a ball and fastened to the back of the head.

hit-and-run driver (line 148–9): a driver of a car who hits someone and drives away without stopping.

gruffly (line 154): in a low and rough voice.

paralysed (line 155): to have no feeling in (a part of) their body, and be unable to move.

to beckon (line 166): to signal to someone to come to you.

LANGUAGE PRACTICE

A

Replace the words underlined with an expression from the text based on the word(s) given in brackets. Make any necessary grammatical changes.

Example: He suddenly started crying (burst).
       He burst into tears.

1 All the doors in the road were painted green (single).
2 I don't understand it. Carl can't drive, but he's bought a car (even).
3 When Becky arrived, Jeff had already given up and gone home (by).
4 It's not difficult to play the recorder, or rather it's not as difficult to play as the piano (at).
5 We haven't got any milk left (run).
6 Elsa thought that most of what the lecturer said was correct (agree).
7 Waving his arms and shouting, Glyn was trying to make Sara notice him (get).
8 Maria checked all the new words in her dictionary (look).
9 Jack was about 30 when he finally got married (or).
10 Tokyo was certainly the most expensive city we visited in the Far East (without).

B

Supply the missing words. In each case, the first letter(s) of the missing word is (are) given. All these expressions are taken from the text.

1 The twins looked the same, but were completely different in character. Abi was practical, with her f___ firmly on the

g____, while Alice was a dreamer, w____ her h____ in the c____.

2 I know a sh____ c____ we can take, that'll get us back home quicker.

3 When it came back from the mender's, the jacket looked a____ g____ a____ n____.

4 Tess found it difficult to walk in h____ h____, so she bought a pair of l____-u____ b____ instead.

5 'B____ the w____,' she added. 'I saw your brother in town yesterday.'

6 To save whales from extinction, a worldwide b____ on w____-h____ was ordered.

7 Elephants and r____ are often killed for their i____ and h____.

8 Amelia said she wouldn't tell anyone, but she didn't k____ her p____.

9 The p____-b____ who saw the accident were able to give the police a good description of the h____- and -r____ d____.

10 If you don't know someone's phone number, you can look it up in the t____ d____.

C

Questions for discussion

1 What type of person would Vicky get on well with?

2 Which of the environmental issues that Vicky and Pluto discussed do *you* think are important? What other issues might they have talked about?

3 This was a supernatural story. Has anything ever happened to you which has no rational explanation?

The Bad Prawn

GLOSSARY

Prawn (title): a small pink shellfish.
over the moon (line 5): very happy about something.
passed out (line 7): lost consciousness.

with two minutes to spare (line 12): two minutes before something happens.

winked (lines 14 and 114): closed and opened one eye very quickly to signal a joke or a secret.

telly (line 14): a short form for 'television'.

treat (line 16): something special that you enjoy.

vol-au-vent (line 23): a small savoury pastry, filled with cheese, prawns, mushrooms, etc.

burped (line 26): made a noise because air from the stomach was expelled up through the throat.

marble (line 30): a hard, cold, polished stone often used for statues and parts of buildings.

pillars (line 30): thick posts used for supporting buildings.

the warm-up man (line 34): a person (here a man) who prepares the television audience for a live show.

cue-cards (line 35): pieces of card with instructions on them, telling you what to do.

APPLAUD (line 36): to clap your hands together.

CHEER (line 36): to shout loudly to show that you like something.

the host of the show (line 39): the person on a radio or television show who introduces it and talks to the people who appear in it.

people settled themselves down (line 44): they sat down comfortably, and waited for something to begin.

the Amazon (line 50): a large river in Brazil.

John didn't pay much attention (line 51): he didn't watch or listen closely.

to feel sick (line 51): to think or feel you are going to vomit, (line 150), when the food and drink you have swallowed comes back out of the mouth.

shivery (line 54): unable to stop your body shaking with cold or fear.

adverts (line 57): short films which tell the people about things they can buy.

burning up (line 59–60): very hot.

gurgled (line 75): the sound of a liquid being pushed through a narrow space.

Glossary and Language Practice

by heart (line 81): to remember something completely.

braces (line 86): elasticated straps which go over your shoulders and attach to your trousers to keep them up.

Pickpocket (line 91): a person who steals things from people's pockets or bags.

licence (line 99): an official document that gives you permission to do something.

bumps into (line 113): accidentally knocks or hits someone when moving.

aisle (line 121): a long narrow gap between rows of seats or shelves that people can walk along.

His head was pounding (line 124–25): throbbing with pain.

make-up (line 142): the powder, lipstick, mascara etc applied to the face.

mask (line 142): a piece of cloth, wood or other material which you wear over your face so that people cannot see who you really are.

with a thump (line 143): with a loud, dull sound.

jerk (line 157): an insult, someone who is stupid and annoying.

a fake (line 160): not genuine, not real.

LANGUAGE PRACTICE

A

Replace the words underlined with an expression from the text based on the word(s) given in brackets. Make any necessary grammatical changes.

Example: He suddenly started crying (burst).
　　　　　He burst into tears.

1 Phil was really happy when his football team won the match three to nil (moon).
2 There are far too many vehicles on the roads these days (traffic).
3 'It's five to eight. You were almost too late (just).'
4 The new teacher walked in and told us his name (introduce).
5 David and Lisa would always remember the night their daughter was born (forget).

71

6 The man on the desk asked me to <u>sit down</u> (take).
7 Peter learnt <u>every word of</u> the Highway Code before taking his driving test (by).
8 He said <u>his name was</u> Edward (call).
9 'It's not a company car,' said Mr Johnson. 'It <u>belongs to me</u> (own).'
10 Lucy <u>never spoke loudly enough</u> for her mother to hear (softly).

B

Supply the missing words. In each case, the first letter(s) of the missing word is (are) given. All these expressions are taken from the text.

1 It was so hot on the day of the parade that two soldiers p____ o____.
2 The children climbed into bed and s____ th____ d____ for their story.
3 The lecture was so boring that none of the students p____ it much a____.
4 I don't f____ w____. My head aches, my stomach hurts and I think I'm going t____ b____ s____.
5 The actor knew all of Shakespeare's plays b____ h____.
6 Ever since Eric got his p____ l____, he has flown his aeroplane every weekend.
7 'Oh, I'm so sorry,' he said. 'I didn't mean to b____ i____ you.'
8 When the singer finished, the a____ gave her a r____ of a____.
9 Judy spent an hour every morning in front of the mirror, putting on her m____-u____.
10 Sir Jasper spent a million pounds on the painting, only to discover that it was a f____.

C

Questions for discussion

1 What did John learn at the television studio about (a) Silvie Lindemann; (b) himself, and (c) the world of television itself?
2 Is everything on television a fake, or are there some programmes that you can trust?

3 John's 'birthday treat' was a trip to the television studio. If you could have anything at all, what treat would you like for your next birthday?

Lucky Luke

GLOSSARY

global warming (line 1): the problem of the earth's temperature getting warmer and warmer.
to adapt (line 2): to change your behaviour.
sweltering (line 4): extremely hot and uncomfortable.
to get it cut (line 5): to have it cut.
wearily (line 8): sounding tired.
the press (line 10): a general word for the newspapers and magazines.
clear off (line 11): informal, 'go away' or 'leave'.
no comment (line 24): a formal expression used by people who will not answer a journalist's questions.
tabloid (line 28): the tabloid newspapers are small, have short articles and lots of pictures.
to let loose on (line 30): to let someone do what they want or like, probably dangerously.
slam the telephone down (line 31): put the receiver down loudly and angrily.
His face fell (line 33): he suddenly looked sad.
and all that (line 41): and other things, usually that everybody knows about.
snipped (line 45): cut small pieces.
So far so good (line 46): informal, to be happy with the way something is going.
board games (line 55): games played on a square piece of wood or stiff cardboard.
dice (line 56): a small cube with dots on each of its sides, numbering from one to six, used in games.
bloke (line 59): an informal word for 'man'.
receding hairline (line 65): the hair at the forehead begins to fall out.

Paper round (line 72): this is a job of delivering newspapers to houses along a route; usually done by girls or boys.

modelling work (line 73–4): to work as a model.

He made a fortune (line 75): he made a lot of money.

inherited (line 81): to be born with something because your parents have it.

Life for Luke is just one big game (line 87–9): Luke believes that being alive means having fun and enjoying himself.

hit the jackpot (line 90): to win a lot of money or have a lot of success.

parting (line 92): the line on someone's head where the hair is combed in opposite directions.

clippers (line 101): an electrical tool for cutting hair short.

an audition (line 104): an audition is a short performance given by an actor, singer, dancer etc so that the director or producer can decide if they are good enough for a part in a film, musical etc.

we're casting (line 106): we're choosing an actor for a part.

'You bet!' (line 116): 'I certainly have!'

telly (line 117): shortened form for 'television'.

a joyrider (line 118): a joyrider is someone, usually a youth, who steals a car and drives around in it at high speed.

whose whole life is turned upside down (line 118): everything in his life changed.

time machine (line 119): a machine which can take people through time.

episode (line 119): one programme in a series.

till (line 141): the small machine where customers' money is kept.

a trim (line 148): a haircut which takes only a little hair off.

it didn't work out like that (line 155): the result was different.

LANGUAGE PRACTICE

A

Replace the words underlined with an expression from the text based on the word(s) given in brackets. Make any necessary grammatical changes.

Example: He suddenly started crying (burst).

He burst into tears.

1 The older boys all told Edward to <u>go away</u> (off).
2 When she heard the news, <u>she suddenly looked very miserable</u> (fall).
3 Luckily, the shop-keeper didn't <u>make me pay</u> for the vase I knocked over and broke (charge).
4 <u>The reason</u> I'm late is that my car wouldn't start this morning (because).
5 Mrs Pringle was <u>too short</u> to reach the top shelf without a ladder (tall).
6 At her third attempt on the slot machine, Maisie <u>struck lucky</u> and won over £1 million (hit).
7 It was <u>because of</u> his father that Luke managed to get the job in the bank (to).
8 His whole life <u>changed completely</u> after the car accident (turn).
9 '<u>Enjoy yourself</u> in Greece,' I called, as my neighbours set off on holiday (fun).
10 Gill decided to walk to the cinema <u>although it was raining</u> (despite).

B

Supply the missing words. In each case, the first letter(s) of the missing word is (are) given. All these expressions are taken from the text.

1 If g____ w____ continues, the polar ice-caps will melt.
2 Alec wears his hair short at the b____ and s____, but long on t____.
3 Joe's father was bald. When Joe looked at his r____ in the m____ he realised that he, too, was already getting a r____ h____.
4 'Th____ n____ of your b____!' she replied angrily, when the interviewer asked if she intended to have children.
5 T____ newspapers are said to print a____ that are not always completely true.
6 It hadn't rained for over ten weeks. The w____ sh____ was becoming very serious.

7 Two minutes before the end of the football match, Pierce
s____ the w____ g____.
8 Eliza left her job in the supermarket and went to Hollywood,
seeking f____ and f____.
9 The new television s____ was called *Time Rider*. Bo Danton
was in it every week, but each e____ was different.
10 Dick w____ for an a____ at the theatre. It was for the p____
of Hamlet.

C

Questions for discussion

1 Jimmy talks a lot about 'luck'? Is there such a thing as good
and bad luck? Are you superstitious? What superstitions do
you know?
2 If the climate does grow warmer, how might this affect (a)
you; (b) your country; (c) the world?
3 How much do you think a person's haircut tells you about his
or her character? How do you react to someone with extremely
long or extremely short hair?

Dining Out

GLOSSARY

Dining out (title): to eat a meal in a restaurant. '*To dine out on a
story*' [line 167] means to repeat the same story at a party or
dinner, to be interesting.
overpowering (line 2–3): a strong personality.
summoned (line 6): to order someone to come.
red mullet (line 8): a type of sea fish.
a bird of prey (line 13): a bird which kills and eats other birds and
animals.
got back in touch (line 16): to talk to someone after a long time
apart.
this and that (line 20): a variety of things.

charity work (line 23): to raise money for people who are ill, handicapped or very poor.

vague (line 29): unclear, imprecise.

private life (line 29): love, friends and hobbies, rather than work.

she'd got her aunt all wrong (line 38–9): she had misunderstood her aunt.

hilarious (line 43): extremely funny.

make fools of themselves (line 46): to make others think you are silly.

sped off (line 56): to go at great speed.

to get from A to B (line 57): a journey, usually a short one.

eagle-eyes (line 60): eyes like an eagle, which do not miss anything.

flashed past (line 62): went past very quickly.

glinted (line 65): a flash of light.

boardwalks (line 72): a footpath made up of wooden boards.

dunes (line 73): sand hills, near the sea or in the desert.

Eva burst into tears (line 87): she suddenly started crying.

to turn up (line 102): to arrive.

fax (line 103): a letter or document sent electronically from machine to machine along a telephone line.

sniffed (line 103): to breathe in through the nose loudly enough to be heard, often when you are trying to stop crying.

What on earth . . . ? (line 107): an expression used to show the speaker's surprise.

worm (line 114): an insult, a weak or unpleasant person you have no respect for.

sympathetic (line 115): kind and understanding to someone who has had some bad luck.

a beast (line 117): (an insult), an animal.

Get it off your chest (line 124–25): talk about something that is worrying you.

by heart (line 126): to remember something completely.

to grow (line 129): here, it means to develop as a human being.

out of town (line 134): away from home, often on business.

cress (line 145): a small, fast-growing plant with strong tasting leaves used for salads.

spelt something out (line 152): to write or speak each letter in the correct order.

gull (line 161): a large, white seabird.

it tricked the penguin into thinking . . . (line 163): it made the penguin believe.

brought back the food (line 164): vomited.

squawk (line 165): a loud harsh noise made by a bird.

gobbled (line 165): to eat fast and greedily, usually without chewing.

LANGUAGE PRACTICE

A

Replace the words underlined with an expression from the text based on the word(s) given in brackets. Make any necessary grammatical changes.

Example: He <u>suddenly started crying</u> (burst).

            He burst into tears.

1. 'It's over five years <u>since</u> I last ate meat,' said Amy (for).
2. Lucy <u>made a firm decision</u> not to tell her mother about her car accident (determine).
3. She <u>had to meet</u> a lot of people in her job (involve).
4. Although it wasn't easy, Dan finally <u>succeeded in</u> finding a job (manage).
5. '<u>It's my fault</u>,' Carol admitted (blame).
6. I didn't like Thomas when I first met him. It was only later that I discovered I'd <u>misunderstood him completely</u> (wrong).
7. Our new boss watched us the whole time. He <u>always noticed everything</u> we did (miss).
8. Boris <u>didn't know</u> that Eva was married (idea).
9. I felt much better about the argument after I'd <u>spoken about it</u> (chest).
10. After the accident, Tom <u>was more careful</u> when he was driving (take).

B

Supply the missing words. In each case, the first letter(s) of the missing word is (are) given. All these expressions are taken from the text.

1 The rabbit was killed and eaten by a huge b____ of p____.
2 I didn't do anything special on holiday; just th____ a____ th____.
3 The old man in the white car was t____ b____ for the traffic accident.
4 I fell over at the disco and m____ a complete f____ of m____.
5 My parents g____ m____ in a ch____ in 1953, and I was born two years later.
6 'W____ o____ e____ are you doing with that gun?' Ted cried out in surprise.
7 I wouldn't recommend a visit to London in February. You'd be b____ o____ waiting till the summer.
8 When my brother was little he u____ to pr____ he was a dog.
9 The postman pushed the envelopes through the l____ b____.
10 Cyril met the Queen in 1978, and d____ o____ on the s____ for years afterwards.

C

Questions for discussion

1 In your own words, what did Eva do to pay Andrew back for leaving her? Was she justified in doing this?
2 Do you think revenge is ever a good motive for what people do?
3 Eva preferred the quiet of Phillip Island to the noise of Melbourne. What about you? Would you like to live in the country or in a big city? Why?

The Abyss

GLOSSARY

abyss (title): a very deep hole in the ground; also on the edge of something very frightening.

howling (lines 1 and 54): the wind howls when it blows hard and makes a loud noise.

headed (line 2): went towards.

he gave me a lift (line 2): he took me in his car.

like a long lost friend (line 11): (to welcome) a stranger like a friend you haven't seen for a long time.

giggled (line 20): laughed in a childlike way.

to blush (line 28): to go red in the face because of shame or embarrassment.

what brings you to Lanzarote . . . (line 33): why did you come to Lanzarote . . .

exhausted (line 39): very tired, physically and mentally.

irritable (line 43): easily annoyed.

brochure (line 53): a magazine or leaflet which gives information about, for instance, holidays and travel.

the swirling sand (line 59): the sand was moving like a liquid, moving round and round quickly.

lava (line 64): the very hot molten rock that comes out of a volcano.

jagged peaks (line 64): uneven shape, with lots of sharp points.

barren . . . *landscape* (line 68-9): a dry, bare landscape with few or no plants.

It's over. (line 72): It's finished.

being so open (line 76): he is being honest and not trying to hide anything.

the end of the world (line 83): here it refers to a place which is very remote. (line 146): here it means, the worst thing that could happen.

my heart was pounding (line 84-5): it was beating fast and loud because he was frightened.

out of my depth (line 86-7): to feel you do not understand, or you are in a situation where you feel helpless.

four-wheel-drive (line 92): a strong vehicle used for rough ground, powered by all four wheels rather than just two.
more nervous than ever (line 97): the most nervous so far.
spiral pillars (line 110): pillars are thick posts used for supporting a building; spiral means to wind upwards.
glistening (line 113): shining or sparkling, because they are wet.
Gothic (line 134): a grand style of architecture, often used for churches and cathedrals in Europe.
peered (line 136): looked with difficulty, because of the darkness.
splash (line 141): the sound of something heavy hitting or landing in water.

LANGUAGE PRACTICE

A

Replace the words underlined with an expression from the text based on the word(s) given in brackets. Make any necessary grammatical changes.

Example: He suddenly started crying (burst).
　　　　He burst into tears.

1 They packed up the tent and set off in a northerly direction (head).
2 I told them it didn't matter what we ate for breakfast (care).
3 'Why did you choose to visit Australia?' the old man asked the German tourist (bring).
4 We were both so tired, we fell asleep at once (pair).
5 We stayed in Ibiza for three weeks (spend).
6 Mr and Mrs Smythe went to Manchester by train (take).
7 Although she knew a lot about the situation in the office, Mary didn't give her opinion (keep).
8 We intended to fly to Rio, but things didn't happen that way (work/plan).
9 The phone stopped ringing just before Peter could answer it (chance).
10 When her horse broke its leg, Mrs Trent had to shoot it (choice).

B

Supply the missing words. In each case, the first letter(s) of the missing word is (are) given. All these expressions are taken from the text.

1 Jill g____ her sister a l____ to the station in her car.
2 The only red door in the road s____ o____ from all the others.
3 'I'll tell you what happened, but I must warn you, i____ a
   l____ s____.'
4 It was awful! First we got lost miles from anywhere, and then
   it started to rain: th____ were going f____ b____ to w____.
5 Lucy didn't know what was going on. She felt completely
   o____ of her d____.
6 An ordinary car is useless in the desert. What you need is a
   f____ w____ d____.
7 The g____ b____ for the city recommended the restaurant very
   highly.
8 When the temperature dropped, the water t____ t____ ice.
9 Amy sat and watched the r____ of the trees in the still water
   of the lake.
10 'I know you're sad,' said Janet's mother, 'but it's n____ the
   e____ of the w____!'

C

Questions for discussion

1 Michael and Helen found it difficult travelling together. What
   sort of person makes a good travelling companion? What sort
   of person would you hate to travel with?
2 Why did Javier take Michael to the caves? What was he trying
   to do? Was he successful? How do you think Michael felt at
   the end? How would *you* have felt?
3 Michael and Helen were in Europe for 'two months of culture'. Is this your idea of a good holiday? If it is, where would
   you particularly like to visit? If it is not, what type of holiday
   would you prefer?

Mr Armitage

GLOSSARY

pure (line 1): complete, total.

paper (line 1): newspaper.

comics (line 4): magazines containing stories told in pictures, usually for children.

demonstrations (line 5): marches or meetings where people show their support or opposition to something.

that caught Andy's eye (line 7): Andy noticed the article.

hypothermia (line 13): a medical term for when the body temperature drops very low.

maths (line 13): the short word for mathematics. (US math)

surgery (line 20): the room or house where a doctor or dentist works.

He gripped the arms of the chair (line 28): he held on very tightly, because he was frightened.

set to work (line 29): begin a task.

dahlia (line 32): a late-summer flower with a lot of brightly coloured petals.

to put up with (line 41): to tolerate.

nickname (line 42): an informal name, usually taken from how somebody looks, or their real name.

he didn't make a big enough impression . . . (line 43–4): if someone makes an impression they have an important effect on a person or situation. Mr Armitage did neither.

comprehensive school (line 48): a state school where children of all abilities are taught together.

shuddered (line 50): shake with fear, cold or disgust.

rinse your mouth out (line 53): to wash it clean with a mouthful of water or antiseptic.

rags (line 66): pieces of old cloth or clothing.

magnifying glass (line 66): a piece of glass, usually on a handle, used for making objects look bigger than they are.

thimble (line 67): a small metal object used to protect your finger when you are sewing.

tramp (line 69): a person with no home or job, and usually very little money.

Bet he stinks! (line 70): Tel is completely sure that the man smells bad.

dosser (line 75): a slang word for *tramp*.

clear off! (line 79): a slang expression meaning, go away.

a nervous breakdown (line 104): an illness of the mind with very bad depression.

derelict (line 108): a word used for a place or building that is empty, and in a very bad state.

a burial service (line 119): a religious ceremony performed when a dead person is buried in the ground.

frost (line 128): the white covering of ice-crystals which appears on everything outside when it is very cold.

could have done with (line 129): if you 'could do with something' you need it. Mr Armitage needed a greenhouse to keep him warm.

all sorts [of] (line 136): a variety, a selection, a wide range.

LANGUAGE PRACTICE

A

Replace the words underlined with an expression from the text based on the word(s) given in brackets. Make any necessary grammatical changes.

Example: He suddenly starting crying (burst).
          He burst into tears.

1 Elaine noticed a small advertisement for a job in the paper (catch).
2 The old man died of cancer (cause).
3 The new teacher was very strict. 'I will not tolerate bad behaviour,' he said (put).
4 When Alan woke up and remembered what he had said and done, he felt completely ashamed (fill).
5 Fred and Tom lit some old newspapers (fire).
6 John Miles ran down the left wing and kicked the ball at the goal with all his strength (as hard as).

7 After her cat <u>died</u>, Mrs Lewis decided not to get a new pet (death).

8 With only two chapters to go, he sat down and <u>finished reading the book</u> (rest).

9 'The church is on the corner of the main road. <u>It's really easy to find</u>' (miss).

10 There <u>was a wide variety</u> of people at Emma's party (all sorts).

B

Supply the missing words. In each case, the first letter(s) of the missing word is (are) given. All these expressions are taken from the text.

1 A d____ was organised to protest about the p____ new road.

2 The tramp had no f____ a____: in other words, he was homeless.

3 Parents try to teach their children the d____ between r____ and wr____.

4 'Those letters are important, Miss Jones,' the secretary's boss told her. 'I'd like you to s____ to w____ at once.'

5 Pop stars often m____ a b____ i____ on the teenagers who like their music.

6 When he had finished drilling, the dentist told me to r____ my m____ o____.

7 The old cinema was kn____ d____ last year to make way for a new supermarket.

8 The writing on the old document was so small that Iris had to use a m____ g____ to read it.

9 Life today is so stressful, that more and more people suffer from n____ b____.

10 Jean's toothache was so bad that she m____ an a____ to see the d____.

C

Questions for discussion

1 How would you help someone like Mr Armitage to stop him being a tramp? What would you do?

2 Young people are often influenced by their friends to do things

they do not want to do. Is it possible to say no to this? What are the dangers for people who can't say no?

3 Andy was ashamed of himself for stoning the tramp. Did you ever do anything when you were younger that now makes you feel ashamed or embarrassed when you remember it?

The Final Memo

GLOSSARY

Memo (title): a short official letter from one person to others in the same company.

had a word with (line 3): a short conversation with someone, usually about one subject.

to transfer (line 6): to move from one place to another.

Still (line 7): used at the beginning of a sentence like this, it is used to say something is not worth worrying about.

computer operators (line 12–13): people who work on computers.

overalls (line 14): a single piece of clothing, jacket and trousers together, worn over ordinary clothes to protect them from dirt, etc.

for ever (line 14): always.

stockroom (line 18–19): a room in a shop or factory where goods are stored.

single [n.] (line 25): means a small record that has one song on each side.

we play live (line 26): the group plays in front of an audience.

Working in this place pays the rent (line 26–7): he means that he does the job only for the money.

A-levels (line 33): *Advanced* level exams, usually taken at school by 17/18 year-olds.

a heart attack (line 38): when the heart suddenly starts beating very irregularly or stops completely.

burst into the office (line 44–5): to come in very quickly and suddenly.

A place for everything and everything in its place (line 46–7): everything should be put away in its proper place.

motto (line 47): a short phrase which gives a rule for sensible behaviour.

officious (line 52): too full of orders and rules.

things came to a head (line 53): to come to a climax.

running out of paper (line 55-6): soon there would be no paper left.

grumbled (line 59): complained.

winked (line 67): closed and opened one eye very quickly to signal a joke or a secret.

Just like the [good] old days (line 67-8): the better days of the past.

a rebel (line 70): someone who doesn't believe in the values of their society, parents, etc.

act of defiance (line 70): not to do what someone tells you.

canteen (line 79): a place in a factory where its employees are served food.

floppy (line 80): limp, not stiff.

bog paper (line 85): is a vulgar term for 'toilet paper'.

Trevor was standing in for him (line 91-2): Trevor was doing Mr Grimble's job while he was on holiday.

trolley (line 94): an object with wheels for transporting things from place to place.

It's come to this! (line 99): 'things have got this bad!'

gasped (line 108): took a sharp intake of breath, because of shock.

She turned on Mrs Brady (line 120): she shouted angrily at Mrs Brady.

glared at (line 131): stared at angrily.

Crystal clear (line 135): 'Yes, I understand completely.'

turned up (line 141): arrived.

The office was in uproar (line 144-45): everyone was being very noisy.

snatched up (line 147): picked up quickly and impatiently.

I resign (line 153): to announce formally that you are leaving your job.

LANGUAGE PRACTICE

A

Replace the words underlined with an expression from the text based on the word(s) given in brackets. Make any necessary grammatical changes.

Lucky Luke and Other Very Short Stories

Example: He suddenly started crying (burst).
　　　　　He burst into tears.

1 John's mother went into school to talk to his teacher about his writing (word).
2 When travelling, Kim checks that her passport is safe time and time again (ever).
3 The phone rang while I was eating (middle).
4 Sally cried and cried when her dog died (stop).
5 When the new headteacher joined the school, everyone knew that things would be different (change).
6 The man told us that we had to take off our hats in the church (insist).
7 Mr Graves was an expert in mountaineering (know/everything).
8 While Mrs Jones was in hospital, Mr Phillips did her job (stand).
9 Working together, we managed to complete the jigsaw puzzle in less than an hour (between).
10 Pat arrived at work at six o'clock every morning (get).

B

Supply the missing words. In each case, the first letter(s) of the missing word is (are) given. All these expressions are taken from the text.

1 Dick's n____ d____ n____ has got three dogs. Their barking keeps him awake at night.
2 'It's not a particularly interesting job,' said Sally, 'but it p____ the r____.'
3 Sue's uncle died of a h____ a____ while he was playing tennis.
4 The company's problems c____ t____ a h____ in July, when five of the managers were sacked.
5 Suddenly, the man t____ o____ me and began shouting angrily.
6 John Doe was born in New York, and lived there a____ his l____.
7 'I think you're lying to me,' said the man. 'I don't b____ a w____ you're saying.'

8 Everyone was so angry about the planned closure of the hospital that the meeting was soon i___ u___.
9 'Who was r___ f___ tearing this book?' asked Miss Green
crossly.
10 With unemployment so high, he was reluctant to r___ from
his job.

C

Questions for discussion

1 Mrs Snape and Mr Arnold were very different types of bosses.
Whose office would you prefer to work in? Why? In whose
office, do you think, the best work would be produced?
2 What is the worst job you have ever done? What is the worst
job you can imagine doing?
3 What advice would you give to a child who wanted to leave
school to join a band?

Fireworks

GLOSSARY

Fireworks (title): fireworks are small objects filled with chemicals
which burn with bright colours and often make a loud noise.
Firework Night or Guy Fawkes' Night is celebrated in Britain
on 5 November.
display (line 8): a show, or a public event.
His heart began to pound (line 9): his heart began to beat loudly
with fear.
tucked up (line 17): to push sheets and blankets tightly around a
person in bed.
cot (line 17): a small enclosed bed for babies and infants.
Miriam shrugged (line 20): she lifted the shoulders in a gesture
which meant that she didn't care what he did.
the baby alarm (line 27): a small listening device, so that you can
hear your baby from another part of the house.
Catherine Wheels (line 34): fireworks which spin round.

Roman Candles (line 35): fireworks which give out a stream of gold-coloured sparks.

rockets (line 36): fireworks which fly into the sky and explode.

As far as he was concerned (line 37): in his opinion.

swatting at (line 38): hitting at an insect with a quick, swinging movement of the hand.

wasp (line 40): a black and yellow striped insect with a painful sting.

That's the price we have to pay (line 41–2): there is a negative side to many things that seem positive and good.

the hottest on record (line 48): the highest temperatures ever recorded.

You'd better come out now (line 61–2): if someone says, 'You'd [had] better', they are giving strong advice or a warning.

childish (line 66): this is the negative word meaning 'like a child'. The positive word is 'childlike.'

slammed (line 68): closed the oven door with a bang.

squeezed (line 74): he held her hand firmly.

for Heaven's sake! (line 78): an expression used when someone is feeling annoyed or impatient.

spectacular (line 88): very impressive and dramatic.

deafening (line 89): extremely loud.

trembling (line 93): shivering with fear.

acrid (line 95): strong, sharp and unpleasant.

shed (line 102): a small building used for storing things like garden tools.

to turn into (line 103): to change from one thing into another.

gunpowder (line 107): a substance used to make fireworks and explosives.

That was a laugh! (line 112): an ironic expression meaning something is *not* funny.

to set light to (line 119): to make something start burning.

blew off the door (line 124): pulled the door from its hinges.

went off (line 126): 'to go off' means 'to explode' here.

scars (line 133): scars are the marks on the skin which remain when a cut or burn has healed.

Adolescence (line 134): the period in your life from about 12 to 18.

he bumped into Miriam (line 143): he met her by chance.

to expose them (line 148): to show something.
I just can't cope with (line 172): I feel helpless, out of control, and
    unable to carry on.
dazzling (line 180): extremely bright.

LANGUAGE PRACTICE

A

*Replace the words underlined with an expression from the text based
on the word(s) given in brackets. Make any necessary grammatical
changes.*

Example: He suddenly started crying (burst).
            He burst into tears.

1 'What about going to France for your holiday?' said Michel
    (why).
2 'I'll be really quick,' said Tracey as she dashed inside
    (minute).
3 In my opinion, the less exercise I have to take, the better
    (concerned)!
4 Why bake your own cakes when you can buy them at the
    baker's (point)?
5 'Sharon's so selfish,' said Alice. 'She only thinks about herself'
    (all).
6 The film is going to start very soon (about).
7 It'll probably rain tomorrow (expect).
8 No matter how many times I asked, he wouldn't tell me what
    happened (refuse).
9 'You should put on your coat. It's freezing outside' (better).
10 Danny didn't learn to drive until he was thirty-five years old
    (before).

B

*Supply the missing words. In each case, the first letter(s) of the missing
word is (are) given. All these expressions are taken from the text.*

1 On 5 N____ every year in Britain, a lot of people have f____
    at home, or go to f____ d____.

2 Susan t____ her daughter u____ in bed, said 'Good Night',
   and closed the door.
3 Being lost in the forest was bad; the rain made it e____ w____.
4 Losing all his teeth was the p____ he h____ to p____ for all
   the sweets he ate.
5 There had never been a hurricane like it. The wind-speed was
   the highest o____ r____.
6 Mr Davies bought the old school and t____ it i____ a hotel.
7 When Alan wanted to start the fire, he took a b____ of m____
   from his pocket, and s____ l____ to the paper and twigs.
8 There were only three survivors from the aeroplane crash.
   They were all very l____ to b____ a____.
9 The operation left him with a big s____ on his stomach.
10 Mrs Lewis sometimes found it hard to c____ w____ the children when her husband was away at sea.

C

Questions for discussion

1 David is terrified of fireworks. Is there anything you are really
   frightened of? Why?
2 Who did you feel more sorry for, David or Miriam? Why?
   Was Miriam right to leave? If they came to you for advice
   about their marriage, what would you say to them?
3 In Britain, we have fireworks on 5 November. When do you
   have fireworks? Why?

The Shikara Man

GLOSSARY

The Shikara Man (title): a 'shikara' is a type of Kashmiri boat or
   'ferry' pushed with a long pole, which is used to take people
   across stretches of water.
on the other hand (line 10): this is used to introduce an opposite
   fact or way of behaving.
a houseboat (line 15): a boat in which people can live.

reasonable (line 17): good value for money.

Top class (line 19): of the highest quality.

cockroaches (line 22): large brown insects that often live in dirty kitchens.

mouses (line 22): the plural of 'mouse' is 'mice'. Akbar thinks that 'mice' are a different animal completely.

the snow-capped Himalayas (line 38): the tops of the mountains are covered with snow at the top.

This is the life (line 40): an informal expression used when everything in your life is perfect.

You can say that again (line 41): an informal expression used when you agree completely with the other person's last statement.

Apparently (line 46): you say 'apparently' to show that you are not sure if something is true.

Maharajah (line 46): an Indian nobleman.

bargains (line 59): things which are good value for money and/or cheaper than their normal price.

Jack of all Trades (line 62): someone who is able to do many different jobs.

mood (line 76): the way you feel at a particular moment.

glinted (line 82): to reflect a flash of light very quickly.

absent-mindedly (line 87): without being aware of what he was doing.

sheep (line 100): if you call people 'sheep', you are criticising them for all copying what one person does.

flickering (line 108–9): a flame or light burning unsteadily.

disturbance (line 123): something that upsets the normal quiet atmosphere.

tangled up in the weeds (line 127): caught in the underwater plants.

He's shaved his head (line 137): he's cut off all his hair with a razor.

in mourning (line 138): to dress or behave in a certain way because someone has died.

gruffly (line 153): in a low and rough voice.

gleamed (line 165): something 'gleams' when a light is shone on it, if it is shiny and clean.

He frowned (line 179): when you 'frown' your eyebrows come together. People frown when they are angry or puzzled.

lice (line 189): lice are small insects which live on the skin of people and bite the skin to drink blood. The singular is 'louse'. Akbar has made the same mistake with 'louse'/'lice', as he made with 'mouse'/'mice'.

LANGUAGE PRACTICE

A

Replace the words underlined with an expression from the text based on the word(s) given in brackets. Make any necessary grammatical changes.

Example: He suddenly started crying (burst).
　　　　　　He burst into tears.

1 You have to be careful when you climb up a ladder at my age (care).
2 It's expensive to fly to Sri Lanka for a holiday, but then again it's cheap to live once you get there (on/hand).
3 Pete's dad collected him from the station (pick).
4 There's a lot of banging and crashing coming from the garage. Do you know what's happening (go)?
5 He had a son who was twelve years old (year).
6 You amaze me! I'm at a loss for words (say).
7 Why don't we go swimming this afternoon (let)?
8 Vivian apologised for breaking the plate, and offered to pay for a new one (sorry).
9 Anne thought it would be a good idea to have dinner before the play started (suggest).
10 When he heard about the trip, he started to smile (break/ grin).

B

Supply the missing words. In each case, the first letter(s) of the missing word is (are) given. All these expressions are taken from the text.

1 The health inspectors closed the restaurant after they found c＿＿ and m＿＿ in the kitchens.

94

2 Ralph leant back in his deckchair, sipped his lemonade and closed his eyes. 'Th____ i____ the l____,' he said to himself happily.

3 The sun glistened on the s____-c____ mountains.

4 Michael can turn his hand to anything. He's a real J____ o____ a____ T____.

5 The h____ on the Dal Lake were b____ by the British, because the M____ wouldn't sell them any l____.

6 The restaurant was recommended in their g____ b____.

7 They weren't ready to order their meal, so they s____ the waiter a____.

8 You know when women on Crete are i____ m____. They w____ black.

9 It rained all morning, but the sun c____ o____ after lunch. Then it cl____ o____ again in the evening.

10 Vinny likes his hair short. He h____ it cl____ every three weeks.

C

Questions for discussion

1 Why did Joe and Mark take a trip around India? Who do you think was better prepared for their time in Kashmir?

2 If you had to describe Akbar to someone, what could you say about (a) his appearance; (b) his character and (c) his life? Do you think you would like him? Why/why not?

3 Akbar didn't like guide books. Why not? When can they be useful? Do you use a guide book when you visit somewhere new?

'Patata'

GLOSSARY

patata (title): the Italian word for 'potato'.
a family joke (line 13): something that was only funny to those within the family.

Shanti had put a little money aside (line 21): he had saved some money.

she went mad! (line 30): she acted in an extravagant and foolish way.

CDs (line 30): compact discs; shiny discs on which something, usually music, has been recorded.

saris (line 31): long thin pieces of material worn around the body, usually by Indian women.

incense (line 31): a substance burnt for its sweet-smelling smoke, often used for religious ceremonies.

Bollywood (line 33): there is a large film industry in Bombay. The name 'Bollywood' comes from *B*ombay and *H*o*llywood*.

baggage allowance (line 35): the weight of the bags and suitcases you can take onto an aeroplane before paying extra.

so-called (line 43): you think the following words are misleading or incorrect.

Fruit 'n Veg Emporium (line 43): Fruit and Vegetable Emporium, i.e. a greengrocer's. 'Emporium' is a formal word for 'shop'.

he couldn't speak English, let alone Hindi (line 48): the informal expression 'let alone' is used after a statement, often negative, to indicate that the following statement will be even more true.

the shop-keeper burst out laughing (line 57): he suddenly started to laugh.

a know-all (line 74): someone who thinks they know more than everyone else. An informal expression.

roared with laughter (line 75): laughed very noisily.

at the tops of their voices (line 83): as loudly as they could.

You are abroad now (line 87): you are in a foreign country now.

no manners (line 89): rude and badly behaved.

the ignition (line 94): the part where you turn the key so the engine starts.

garage (line 100): a place where you can get your car repaired.

practical (line 103): good at solving ordinary problems, particularly those which need work with the hands.

a scooter (line 105): a small light motorcycle.

Shanti shrugged (line 117–8): he raised his shoulders to show that he didn't know.

the bonnet (line 127): the hinged metal cover above the engine of a car, when it is situated at the front. (U.S. Hood)

the exhaust pipe (line 137): the pipe at the back of the car which carries the gases out of the engine.

It was all a trick! (line 146): the whole incident was not how it first appeared.

fallen for (line 149): (here) to believe a trick, or something that is not true.

LANGUAGE PRACTICE

A

Replace the words underlined with an expression from the text based on the word(s) given in brackets. Make any necessary grammatical changes.

Example: He suddenly started crying (burst).
        He burst into tears.

1 The policeman became suspicious when the man said that he wouldn't give his name or address (refuse).
2 John saved a little money each week. At the end of a year he bought himself a new racing-bike (put).
3 Although he had forgotten his key, Brian was able to climb in through an upstairs window (manage).
4 When Mr Snelgrove fell over on the ice all the children suddenly started to laugh (out).
5 Despite her brave smile, you could tell that the woman was worried (although).
6 Christopher was singing in the bath as loudly as he could (top).
7 He was hurrying so much, he forgot to take his wallet (in).
8 If you want to arrive before the film starts, how about taking a taxi to the cinema? (why).
9 The vet said Alex's dog is perfectly all right (wrong).
10 I told you, I don't like alcohol. I don't drink wine, and I certainly don't drink whisky (let).

B

Supply the missing words. In each case, the first letter(s) of the missing word is (are) given. All these expressions are taken from the text.

1 Zoe buys fresh f____ and v____ from the market every day.
2 Howard and Jenny flew to Barcelona and h____ a c____ to drive around in.
3 Although it cost a lot, Mark thought his computer was w____ e____ penny.
4 Wolfgang spoke four languages: E____, F____, I____ and, of course, G____.
5 The joke was so good, Andy th____ back his h____ and r____ with l____.
6 If there was one thing that Mrs Miller hated it was rude little children with n____ m____.
7 Edgar turned the k____ in the i____ and s____ the car. Then he drove off quickly.
8 Miranda had wanted to be an astronaut all her life, but it was a w____ which never c____ t____.
9 The bus p____ u____ next to us, and we all got on.
10 Emily sat up in bed, opened her eyes and stared at the ghost i____ h____.

C

Questions for discussion

1 What does Chandra like about Rome? What does she dislike about Bombay? Was she right to blame herself for falling for the thieves' trick?
2 Why do you think Shanti reacted as he did when he realised their car had been stolen? How would you have reacted?
3 Chandra was angry with the children for behaving badly abroad. Do you feel you represent your country when you are abroad? Does this make you behave any differently?

Origami

GLOSSARY

Origami (title): 'origami' is the Japanese art of folding paper to make models of animals and objects.

to live on (line 4): to buy everything he needed.

ancient ruins (line 9): the parts of very old buildings that remain when the rest has fallen down or been destroyed.

parade (line 10): a procession, a line of celebrating people.

tea plantations (line 11): areas of land where tea is grown.

the going-rate (line 15–16): the average amount you could expect something to cost.

rupees (line 16): the Sri Lankan currency.

put it (line 19): expressed it, said.

a bargain (line 20): something that is good value for money.

a sharp intake of breath (line 28–9): to breathe in quickly and noisily, usually to indicate someone is shocked or annoyed; 'to gasp' (line 32) is a stronger expression.

turn up (line 37–8): to arrive.

on the dot (line 38–9): an informal expression meaning at exactly the time given.

to build up their confidence (line 45): to make their confidence grow.

At school (line 49): '*at* school' means you are a pupil; '*in* the school' means 'in the building'.

growled (line 51): said in a low, rough, angry voice.

the palm of his hand (line 52): the palm is the flat area on the inside of the hand.

to make a note (line 56): to write something down quickly, so that you have a record of it.

errors (line 57): mistakes.

exercise books (line 60): small books with blank pages which pupils and students write in.

a Japanese saying (line 64): a saying is a memorable sentence that a lot of people say. It often gives you advice or tells you something about human experience.

after all (line 70): at the end of a sentence 'after all' is used when
   something you did not think was true, is in fact true.
a crane (line 70): a large bird with a long neck and long legs.
from a single sheet of blue paper (line 71): with one piece of blue
   paper.
window sill (line 72): a ledge at the bottom of a window both
   inside and outside.
eager (line 76): keen; they wanted to start talking.
The nail that stands up is hammered down (line 79–80): if you try
   to be different from other people you will be knocked back
   into place.
conform (line 84): to behave like everyone else.
blushed (line 91): went red in the face because of shame or embarrassment.
joke (line 103): a very short, funny story.
at their ease (line 104): relaxed and comfortable.
fluently (line 104): accurately, clearly, and without hesitation.
He cleared his throat (line 109): he coughed once to make it easier
   to speak.
a sweet tooth (line 110): to like eating sweet things.
crockery (line 111): 'crockery' is the cups, saucers, bowls and
   plates you use at mealtimes.
black humour (line 113): jokes about subjects such as death or
   illness.
dragon (line 116): a mythical flying creature which is said to
   breathe fire.
Happy Birthday . . . and many happy returns (lines 123–24): a
   greeting spoken to people who are celebrating their birthday,
   and wishing them many more to follow.
bowing (line 125): to bend your body towards someone as a formal
   greeting or mark of respect.
Aquarius (line 129): a person whose sign of the zodiac is Aquarius
   is born between mid-January and mid-February.
fortune-telling (line 131): the art of predicting your future by looking at your palm, interpreting the position of the stars, etc.
I-Ching (line 132): an ancient Chinese system of telling the future
   using a set of sticks or coins, and a text book.
The wrapping was a work of art (line 135): 'a work of art' is usually

a painting or a sculpture. The parcel is wrapped with artistic
perfection.

bows (line 137): 'bows' are ribbons tied in a decorative knot.

chopsticks (line 144): a pair of thin sticks which people in the Far
East use to eat their food with.

an insular people (line 150): people who do not want to meet new
people or consider new ideas.

surveys (line 151): a list of questions to get information about the
opinions of people.

It is . . . a shame (line 152): an informal expression used to show
regret.

stay in touch (line 157): to write or phone when you do not see
someone regularly.

wallet (line 163): a small flat folded case, usually made of leather,
to keep banknotes and credit cards.

Why had they cheated him? (line 166): why had they behaved
dishonestly to him?

swan (line 175): a large bird with a long, curved neck that lives
on rivers and lakes.

LANGUAGE PRACTICE

A

*Replace the words underlined with an expression from the text based
on the word(s) given in brackets. Make any necessary grammatical
changes.*

Example: He suddenly started crying (burst).
        He burst into tears.

1 If it doesn't rain, we'll all go to the zoo (long).
2 Eric got home, heard the message from Amy on his answer
  machine and called her back immediately (at).
3 I thought Phillip was a doctor, but I was completely mistaken.
  He's a journalist (get/all).
4 The plane touched down at Kennedy airport at exactly eleven
  o'clock (dot).
5 The secretary wrote down my name and phone number, and
  said that Mr Jones would call me back later (make).

6 Alex put the letter in his pocket and <u>forgot all</u> about it (no more).

7 Although Ron and Louise have been going to German lessons for over a year, they never seem <u>relaxed</u> in class (at).

8 At the end of the holiday, Doug and Ed swapped addresses and promised <u>not to lose contact</u> with each other (stay).

9 I don't understand why Molly needs two cars. <u>It just isn't logical</u> (sense).

10 When she arrived in Berlin, she decided to explore <u>the whole</u> city (inch).

B

Supply the missing words. In each case, the first letter(s) of the missing word is (are) given. All these expressions are taken from the text.

1 Students are expected to l___ o___ £3,000 a year, which is far too little money.

2 The g___-r___ for a guitar lesson these days is £15 an hour.

3 Donald stayed in all evening waiting for Clare. She finally t___ u___ at midnight.

4 Before the lesson started, Miss Miles played some simple word-games with the students, to help them b___ u___ their c___.

5 I've never seen anyone eat so much chocolate as Kenny. He's got a real s___ t___.

6 H___ Birthday, Thomas, and m___ h___ r___!

7 We went to Corinth last year, to look at the a___ r___ of Greece.

8 Ian pl___ an a___ in the local newspaper when he wanted to sell his motor-bike.

9 The lecturer looked up, c___ his th___, and began to talk in a loud voice.

10 I don't believe in f___-t___. There is no way to predict the future.

C

Questions for discussion

1 What differences does John recognise exist between British and Japanese culture? Many people say the British are reserved: do you think other nationalities have certain characteristics?

2 Do you believe it is possible to see into the future? What methods of fortune-telling do you know?

3 Do you know how to make any model animals or objects? Could you give instructions to someone else as to how to make one?

Memory Lane

GLOSSARY

Memory Lane (title): 'to take a trip down Memory Lane' means to remember a lot of events from the past.

a bill (line 3): a written statement of money that you owe for gas, electricity, etc.

exotic (line 5): something that is unusual and interesting, usually from a far-away country.

lychees (line 6): a far eastern fruit with a red skin, sweet white flesh, and a large stone.

acquaintance (line 10): a person you have met, but do not know well enough to call a friend.

puzzled (line 24): confused.

muggers (line 25): a person who attacks someone on the street to steal money from them.

When I came round (line 26): when I regained consciousness.

Amnesia (line 27): loss of memory.

A loony (line 31): an informal term for someone you think is mad (abbreviation of 'lunatic').

alphabetically (line 40): to make a list in the order of the letters of the alphabet.

rustled (line 48): something thin and dry, like paper or leaves, rustles when it is gently moved.

After all (line 52–3): at the beginning of the sentence, 'after all' is used to support or explain something you have just said.

divorce (line 55): 'divorce' is the formal end to a marriage.

bitterly (line 58): angrily, very disappointedly.

tingled (line 59): a slight prickling feeling, like feeling cold. You can tingle with anticipation or excitement.

spine (line 60): part of the body, the backbone.

Miriam pursed her lips (line 65): she pulled her lips into a small, tight circle. You often do this when you disapprove of something.

scowled (line 65): to frown and move your mouth to show anger or dislike.

betrayal (line 70): this is the noun from 'to betray'. To lie to or hurt someone who trusts you.

to get 'into television' (line 75): to get any kind of job in television.

barren hills (line 83): dry, bare hills with few plants and no trees.

monasteries (line 84): buildings in which monks live.

The company (line 86): the pleasant state of being with others so that you do not feel lonely.

a word I can't quite make out (line 94): a word I can't read properly.

monks (line 108): members of a male religious community who live away from the world.

maroon robes (line 108): dark red, loose-fitting clothes, which cover the body and reach down to the ground.

digital watch (line 119): a battery-operated watch which shows the time by numbers rather than with hands.

Wall Street (line 120): the banking and financial centre of New York.

to take offence (line 128): to feel upset because someone has been rude to you.

selfless (line 129): thoughtful, considerate of others.

to start a family (line 138): to have children.

tiny organisms in the water (line 140–41): very small plants or animals you can only see through a microscope.

fertile (line 145): able to have babies.

screwed the letter up into a ball (line 150): squeezed and twisted the letter tightly until it was shaped like a ball.

LANGUAGE PRACTICE

A

Replace the words underlined with an expression from the text based on the word(s) given in brackets. Make any necessary grammatical changes.

Example: He suddenly started crying (burst).
         He burst into tears.

1 When she regained consciousness she found herself lying in an unfamiliar room (come).
2 Although the weather forecast was good, he took his umbrella (nevertheless).
3 'Sorry, but I can't come this evening after all' (afraid).
4 William and Nancy liked each other a lot (get).
5 We usually eat at a restaurant in town on Friday night (more/not).
6 Simon took an extra squash racquet with him because it was possible that Ted would forget his again (in).
7 Joshua's handwriting is awful! I can hardly read a single word (out).
8 Just as we were beginning to enjoy it, the film ended suddenly (come/end).
9 Janice was upset by his comment about women (take/offence).
10 Five years after they married, they thought about having children (family).

B

Supply the missing words. In each case, the first letter(s) of the missing word is (are) given. All these expressions are taken from the text.

1 My last gas b____ was for £200.
2 Joe was a____ by m____ last night. They stole all his money.
3 Names in the telephone book are all l____ a____.
4 Paris is the c____ of France.

5 The lamb curry m_____ a w_____ ch_____ to his diet of bread and water.

6 The h_____ a_____ at the top of the mountain gave Briony a headache.

7 Peter's d_____ w_____ is so accurate, it always tells the right time.

8 Darren and Patsy g_____ m_____ in a church in 1985. Three years later they s_____ a f_____. Now they have four children.

9 In Nepal you should never drink u_____ w_____, no matter how thirsty you are.

10 Tony s_____ the paper u_____ and threw it into the rubbish bin.

C

Questions for discussion

1 Have you ever done something that you didn't want to, to avoid hurting another person's feelings? What? Are you glad you did it?

2 Is tourism a good thing or a bad thing? Do you think it helps us to understand people from different cultures?

3 What five pieces of advice would you give to a friend who was about to go on a trip to the Himalayas?